The Saladin was a wheeled vehicle produced in 1958 with a 76mm (3in) cannon. The AMX-13 has a 90mm (3.5in) cannon, and weighs 15 tonnes. The French also introduced the Panhard 8-wheeled EBR armoured car, with a 90mm (3.5in) cannon and a driver's compartment at both ends, with a crew of four. Later requirements led to Britain introducing the Combat Vehicle Reconnaissance (Tracked) Scorpion, the Scimitar and the Combat Vehicle Reconnaissance (Wheeled) Fox. France also produced the successful AMX-10 series, the Renault VBC-90 and the Panhard ERC-90 series with a variation of guns and turrets.

The Soviet reconnaissance vehicles include the BTR, BMP and PT76, as well as the BRDM, which has a variety of weapons fits. The Russians also have the PT76 light tank, which has a 76mm (3in) gun and a swimming capability, and one of the mainstays of their battalions is the T-62, also used in a reconnaissance role.

With the development of more sophisticated delivery systems capable of pinpoint accuracy, tank manufacturers have had to continue to develop better protection, communications, firepower and mobility, as well as more automatic systems to protect crews and ensure that they are able to carry out their assignments.

The Thyssen Henschel 400 6 × 6 is the latest in the German range of APCs which can be fitted with a vast range of armaments

Abbreviations

AA: anti-aircraft
ACRV: armoured command and reconnaissance vehicle
AFSV: armoured fire-support vehicle
AFV: armoured fighting vehicle
AGV: assault gun vehicle
AIFV: armoured infantry fighting vehicle
AP: armour piercing
APC: armoured personnel carrier
APDS: armour-piercing discarding sabot
APERS-T: anti-personnel tracer
APFSDS: armour-piercing fin-stabilised discarding sabot
APM: anti-personnel mine
ARP: anti-radiation projectile

ARSV: armoured reconnaissance scout vehicle
ARV: armoured recovery vehicle
ASV: ammunition supply vehicle
ATG: anti-tank gun
ATGW: anti-tank guided weapon
ATM: anti-tank mine
ATTS: automatic tank target system
CEV: combat engineer vehicle
CP: concrete-piercing
CPV: command-post vehicle
CVR(T): combat vehicle, reconnaissance (tracked)
CVR(W): combat vehicle, reconnaissance (wheeled)
DDU: digital display unit

DHSS: data handling subsystem
EMG: externally mounted gun
EOD: explosive ordnance disposal
ERV: emergency rescue vehicle
FACE: field-artillery computer equipment
FAST: fully automatic scoring/target system
FG: field gun
FH: field howitzer
FLIR: forward-looking infrared
FROG: free rocket over ground
FSCV: fire-support combat vehicle
GCE: gun control equipment
GH: gun/howitzer
GPMG: general purpose machine gun
GPO: gun position officer
GPS: gunners primary sight

GW: guided weapon
HAWK: homing all-the-way killer
HB: heavy barrel
HCHE: high capacity high-explosive
HE: high explosive
HEAT: high explosive anti-tank
HEAT-MP: high explosive anti-tank multi-purpose
HEAT-T-MP: high explosive anti-tank tracer multi-purpose
HEDP: high explosive dual purpose
HEI: high explosive incendiary
HEIT: high explosive incendiary tracer
HEP: high explosive plastic
HESH: high explosive squash head
HPT: high pressure test

HVAP: high velocity armour piercing
HVAPDS-T: high velocity armour piercing discarding sabot tracer
HVAPFSDS: high velocity armour piercing fin-stabilised discarding sabot
HVAP-T: high velocity armour piercing tracer
IAFV: infantry armoured fighting vehicles
IFCS: integrated fire-control system
IFV: infantry fighting vehicle
IR: infrared
IRBM: inter range ballistic missile
ITV: improved TOW vehicle
LAAG: light anti-aircraft gun
LADS: light air defence system
LAV: light assault vehicle *or* light armoured vehicle
LAW: light anti-tank weapon
LLLTV: low light level television
LMG: light machine gun
LVA: landing vehicle, assault
LVT: landing vehicle, tracked
LVTC: landing vehicle, tracked command
LVTE: landing vehicle, tracked engineer
LVTP: landing vehicle, tracked personnel
LVTR: landing vehicle, tracked recovery
MAC: medium armoured car
MBT: main battle tank

MEV: medical evacuation vehicle
MG: machine gun
MRS: multiple rocket system
MT: mechanical time
MTI: moving target indication
MTSQ: mechanical time and superquick
MULE: modular universal laser equipment
MV: muzzle velocity
NATO: North Atlantic Treaty Organisation
NBC: nuclear, biological, chemical
OP: observation post
OT: operational test
PAR: pulse acquisition radar
PCB: printed circuit board
PD: point detonating
PFHE: pre-fragmented high explosive

RAP: rocket-assisted projectile
RATAC: radar for field artillery fire
RDF/LT: rapid deployment force light tank
RMG: ranging machine gun
ROF: Royal Ordnance Factory *or* rate of fire
ROR: range only radar
RPV: remotely-piloted vehicle
RSAF: Royal Small Arms Factory
SADARM: sense and destroy armour
SAL: semi-active laser
SAM: surface-to-air missile
SHORAD: short range air defence system
SMG: sub-machine gun

SPAAG: self-propelled anti-aircraft gun

SPAG: self-propelled assault gun

SPATG: self-propelled anti-tank gun

SPAW: self-propelled artillery weapon

SRG: shell replenishment gear

STAFF: smart target activated fire and forget

SWAT: special warfare armoured transporter

TACOM: tank automotive command

TADS: target acquisition and designation system

TAS: tracking adjunct system

TCU: tactical control unit

TD: tank destroyer

TES: target engagement system

TIS: thermal imaging system

TOGS: thermal observation and gunnery system

TTS: tank thermal sight

VHIS: visual hit indicator system

WAPC: wheeled armoured personnel carrier

WFSV: wheeled fire support vehicle

WMRV: wheeled maintenance and recovery vehicle

One of the world's latest main battle tanks, the Hyundai/General Dynamics Type 88, has been deployed with the South Korean Army since 1987

16

Type 69-II

Country of origin: China
Type: main battle tank
Crew: four
Combat weight: 36,500/37,000kg (80,467/81,570lb)
Dimensions: length with gun forward 8.657m (28.4ft), 6.243m (20.48ft), hull only; width 3.298m (10.82ft); height including AA gun at full elevation 3.909m (12.825ft); ground clearance 0.425m (1.4ft)
Armament system: one 10mm (3.94in) rifled gun; two 7.62mm (0.31in) Type 59T machine guns; one 12.7mm (0.5in) Type 54 AA machine gun; the turret is electro-hydraulically powered, the main gun stabilised in elevation
Armour: cast and welded steel varying between 20-203mm (0.79-8in) thickness
Powerplant: 435kW (583hp) Model 12150L-7BW diesel engine
Performance: road speed 50km/h (31.1mph); road range 440km (273 miles); fording 1.4m (4.6ft); gradient 60%; side slope 40%; vertical obstacle 0.8m (31.5in); trench 2.7m (8.9ft); internal fuel unrevealed

The Type 69-II improved model, Model 1, optimised for the export market and fitted with a rifled rather than smooth-bore main armament, has a number of options in the fire-

control system

Type 59

Country of origin: China
Type: main battle tank
Crew: four
Combat weight: 36,000kg (79,365lb)
Dimensions: length with gun forward 9m (29.53ft), 6.04m (19.82ft) hull only; width 3.27m (10.73ft); height overall 2.59m (8.5ft), to turret top only 2.4m (7.87ft)
Armament system: one 100mm (3.94in) Type 59 rifled gun stabilised in elevation +17°, depression −4°, but not in azimuth (360°); two 7.62mm (0.31in) Type 59 machine guns; one 12.7mm (0.5in) Type 54 AA machine gun; the turret is electro-hydraulically powered, and an optical fire-control system is fitted
Armour: cast and welded steel varying between 20-203mm (0.79-8in)
Powerplant: 388kW (520hp) Model 12150L V-12 diesel engine
Performance: road speed 50km/h (31.1mph); road range 440km (273 miles) on internal fuel of 815 litres (179 Imp gal) or 600km (373 miles) with auxiliary fuel

This is the Chinese derivative of the USSR's T-54, and is currently the main gun tank fielded by the armies of China

GIAT AMX-30

Country of origin: France
Type: main battle tank
Production: deliveries commenced in 1967
Crew: four
Combat weight: 36,000kg (79,350lb) loaded
Dimensions: length, gun forward, 9.48m (31ft 1in), 6.59m (21ft 7in) hull; width 3.10m (10ft 2in); height 2.86m (9ft 4.5in) to top of cupola
Armament system: one 105mm (4.13in) gun, elevation +20°, depression −8°, 50 rounds carried; one 12.5mm (0.5in) MG or 20mm (0.79in) coaxial cannon, 1,050 rounds; one 7.62mm (0.31 in) machine gun on commander's cupola, 2,050 rounds; two × two smoke grenade launchers
Armour: welded and cast steel, varying in thickness between 20-80.8mm (0.79-3.18in)
Powerplant: Hispano-Suiza HS-110, 12-cylinder multi-fuel water-cooled engine developing 720hp at 2,400rpm
Performance: speed 65km/h (40mph); range 600km (373 miles); fuel 970 litres (213 Imp gal)
Ground pressure: 0.77kg/cm² (10.95psi)
History: the AMX-30 is fitted with infrared driving and fighting equipment, while the AMX-30B2 later production variant is also fitted with laser rangefinder and automatic COTAC integrated fire control system. Other variants are the AMX-30 Export Model, the AMX-30S and the AMX-30 Shatine, a SAM version.

Krauss-Maffei/Krupp MaK Leopard 2

Country of origin: West Germany
Type: main battle tank
Production: entered service in 1979
Crew: four
Combat weight: 55,150kg (121,583lb)
Dimensions: length with gun forward 9.688m (31ft 8in), 7.722m (25ft 3in) hull only; width overall including skirts, 3.7m (12ft 1in); height to turret top 2.46m (8ft); ground clearance 0.53m (1ft 8in) front, 0.48m (1ft 6in) rear
Armament system: one 120mm (4.75in) tank gun; one 7.62mm (0.31in) coaxial machine gun; one 7.62mm (0.31in) AA machine gun
Armour: spaced multi-layer type
Powerplant: MTU MB 873 Ka 501 4-stroke, 12-cylinder multi-fuel, exhaust turbocharged, liquid-cooled, developing 1,500hp at 2,600rpm
Performance: speed 72km/h (44.72mph) forward; range 550km (341.5 miles)
Ground pressure: 0.81kg/cm² (11.58psi)
History: the Leopard 2 combines maximum protection with high mobility and enhanced firepower. Two types of ammunition are fired, both fin-stabilised; the APFSDS-T, with an effective range well in excess of 2,000m (1.2 miles), and the HEAT-MP-T. Variants include Swiss and Dutch versions.

The Leopard 2 is a highly protected and formidable MBT with potent firepower

Krauss-Maffei/Krupp MaK Leopard 1

Country of origin: West Germany
Type: main battle tank
Production: first delivery was September 1965
Crew: four
Combat weight: 40,000kg (88,185lb) loaded, 38,700kg (85,319lb) empty
Dimensions: length with gun forward 9.54m (31ft 3in), 7.09m (23ft 3in) hull only; width 3.25m (10ft 8in), 3.4m (11ft 2in) with skirts; height 2.61m (8ft 6in) to periscope
Armament system: one 105mm (4.13in) L7A3 gun, elevation +20°, depression −9° (stabilised), 60 rounds carried; two 7.62mm (0.31in) MGs, coaxial and AA, 5,500 rounds; four smoke dischargers on both sides of turret
Armour: 10-70mm (0.4-2.75in) estimated
Powerplant: MTU MB 838 Ca. M500, 10-cylinder multi-fuel engine, developing 830hp at 2,200rpm
Performance: road speed 65km/h (40mph); range 500km (372 miles), 450km (280 miles) cross-country; fuel 955 litres (209 Imp gal)
Ground pressure: 0.9kg/cm² (12.87psi)
History: the original intention, in the mid-1950s, was for Italy and France to work with Germany on the development of a standard tank, but disagreement led to France building her AMX-30 and Italy the M60A1, although Italy did later purchase the Leopards, as did others.

Israeli Ordnance Corps Merkava Mk 1

Country of origin: Israel
Type: main battle tank
Production: became available in 1979
Crew: four
Combat weight: 56,000kg (123,345lb)
Dimensions: length with gun forward 8.63m (28ft 4in), 7.45m (24ft 5in) hull; width 3.7m (12ft 7in); height 2.64m (8ft 8in) to turret roof
Armament system: one 105mm (4.13in) gun, elevation +20°, depression −8°, 65+ rounds carried; smoke dischargers and 60mm (2.36in) roof-mounted mortar
Armour: cast and welded steel
Powerplant: Continental AVDS-1790-5A V-12 diesel engine developing 900hp at 2,400rpm
Performance: speed 46km/h (28.5mph); range 500km (310 miles); fuel 1,200 litres (263 Imp gal) estimated
History: engine and transmission are positioned at the front, while doors at the rear provide a facility for the quick reloading of ammunition. The relatively small turret is also placed towards the rear. Variants include the Mk 2, with hydropneumatic suspension, and most recently the Mk 3, incorporating a larger-calibre gun, which entered service in 1989.

This excellent MBT reflects the lessons of Israel's recent war-torn past

OTO Melara/Fiat OF-40 Mk 1

Country of origin: Italy
Type: main battle tank
Production: became available in 1981
Crew: four
Combat weight: 43,000kg (94,798lb) loaded, 40,000kg (88,185lb) empty
Dimensions: length with gun forward 9.222m (30ft 3in), 6.893m (22ft 7in) hull only; width 3.51m (11ft 6in) with skirts; height 2.68m (8ft 11in) to commander's sight
Armament system: one 105mm (4.13in) gun, elevation + 20°, depression − 9°, 61 rounds carried; two 7.62mm (0.31in) machine guns, coaxial and AA, 5,500 rounds carried; four smoke dischargers on both sides of the turret
Armour: welded steel
Powerplant: 90° V-10 supercharged multi-fuel engine developing 830hp at 2,200rpm
Performance: speed 60km/h (37.25mph); road range 600km (372 miles); fuel 1,000 litres (220.26 Imp gal)
Ground pressure: 0.86kg/cm² (12.3psi)
History: Fiat developed the engine, while OTO-Melara was responsible for the hull, chassis and armament. A laser rangefinder is standard, together with a roof-mounted SFIM 580B sight. An over-pressure NBC system is fitted.

Since its introduction, the Mk 1 has been improved (Mk 2) and then upgraded (Mk 3)

Mitsubishi Type 61

Country of origin: Japan
Type: main battle tank
Production: vehicles became available in 1962; about 560 Type 61 MTBs were built
Crew: four
Combat weight: 35,000kg (27,160lb) loaded
Dimensions: length with gun forward 8.19m (26ft 10in), 6.3m (20ft 8in) hull only; width 2.95m (9ft 8in)
Armament system: one 90mm (3.54in) Type 61 gun; one 7.62mm (0.31in) M1919A4 coaxial machine gun; one 12.7mm (0.5in) Browning M2HB
Armour: 64mm (2.52in)
Powerplant: Mitsubishi Type 12 HM 21 WT V-12 turbocharged diesel engine developing 600hp at 2,100rpm
Performance: road speed 45km/h (28mph); road range 200km (124 miles)
Ground pressure: 0.95kg/cm² (13.59psi)
History: the first Japanese postwar tank, the Type 61 was built under the direction of the Ground Armaments Directorate at the headquarters of the Japanese Self-Defence Forces. The Type 61 is now obsolete, owing to poor armament and all-round performance. Variants included the Type 67 AVLB and Type 70 ARV; both used the Type 61 chassis.

Now obsolete, the Type 61 bore many American characteristics

Bofors Stridsvagn 103B

Country of origin: Sweden
Type: main battle tank
Production: deliveries began in 1966
Crew: three
Dimensions: length with gun forward 9.8m (32ft 1in), 8.4m (27ft 6in) hull only; width overall 3.6m (11ft 9in); height 2.14m (7ft) to commander's cupola, 2.5m (8ft 2in) with MG; ground clearance 0.5m (1ft 7in) at centre of hull, 0.4m (1ft 3in) at sides of hull
Armament system: one 105mm (4.16in) L7A1 L/62 gun; two 7.62mm (0.31in) coaxial MGs; one 7.62mm (0.31in) AA MG
Armour: welded steel
Powerplant: Rolls-Royce K60 multi-fuel engine developing 240bhp at 3,650rpm and Boeing 365kW (490shp) 553 gas-turbine
Performance: land speed 50km/h (31mph), on water 6km/h (3.7mph); range 390km (192 miles)
Ground pressure: 0.9kg/cm² (12.87psi)
History: the 103B is unique in that it has no turret, the gun being located in the hull, and fed externally from a magazine with a 50-round capacity. The automatic loader enables a fast rate of fire of 15 rounds per minute. Two fixed machine guns are mounted on the left of the turret and can only be loaded externally.

The improved 103C with a Detroit-Diesel 6V-53T

Federal Construction Pz 68

Country of origin: Switzerland
Type: main battle tank
Production: the first production tanks were delivered in 1971
Crew: four
Combat weight: 39,700kg (87,532lb) loaded; 38,700kg (85,319lb) empty
Dimensions: length with gun forward 9.49m (31ft 1in), 6.98m (22ft 11in) hull only; width 3.14m (10ft 4in); height 2.75m (9ft) to cupola
Armament system: one 105mm (4.13in) gun, elevation +21°, depression −10°, 56 rounds carried; two 7.5mm (0.39in) machine guns, coaxial and AA, 5,200 rounds carried; six smoke dischargers
Armour: 60mm (2.36in) maximum
Powerplant: MTU MB 837 V-8 diesel, developing 660bhp at 2,200rpm
Performance: road speed 55km/h (34mph); road range 350km (217 miles); fuel 710 litres (155 Imp gal)
Ground pressure: 0.86kg/cm² (12.3psi)
History: a development of the Pz 61 MBT which, in 1961, had become Switzerland's first home-produced MBT. The Pz 68s have only been supplied to the Swiss army. The improved Mk 2 appeared in 1974, the Mk 3 (with larger turret) in 1978, and the Mk 4 in 1981.

An improved version of the Pz 61, which entered service in 1965

T-80

Country of origin: USSR
Type: main battle tank
Crew: three
Combat weight: 42,000kg (92,593lb)
Dimensions: length with gun forward 9.9m (32.48ft), 7.4m (24.28ft) hull only; width 3.4m (11.155ft); height without AA MG 2.2m (7.22ft); ground clearance 0.38m (1.25ft)
Armament system: one 125mm (4.92in) D-81TM (2A46 Rapira 3) smooth-bore gun/missile launcher stabilised in elevation (+18° to −6°) and azimuth (360°) with 40 rounds including AT-8 'Songster' missiles; one 7.62mm (0.31in) PICT coaxial MG with 2,000 rounds; one 12.7mm (0.5in) NSVT AA MG with 500 rounds and between 8-12 smoke dischargers.
Armour: cast and composite
Powerplant: one 735kW (986hp) gas turbine
Performance: road speed 75km/h (46.6mph); range 400km (249 miles) on internal fuel; fording 1.4m (4.6ft) without preparation and 5.5m (18ft) with snorkel; fuel 1,000 litres (220.26 Imp gal) internal; 400 litres (88 Imp gal) of external fuel in two jettisonable tanks
History: stationed in East Germany, the T80 was of major importance to the Soviet army. Fitted with reactive armour since 1984, the updated M1989 had additional armour protection and improved fire-control systems.

Basically the T-64B without problems

T-72

Country of origin: USSR
Type: main battle tank
Production: the T-72 entered production in 1972
Crew: three
Combat weight: 41,000kg (25,500lb) loaded
Dimensions: length with gun forward 9.2m (30ft 2in), 6.9m (22ft 7in) hull; width overall 4.75m (15ft 7in) with skirts; height 2.37m (7ft 9in); ground clearance 0.47m (1ft 6.5in)
Armament system: one 125mm (4.92in) gun; one 7.62mm (0.31in) coaxial gun; one 12.7 (0.5in) AA gun
Powerplant: V-12 diesel (V-46), developing 780hp at 3,000rpm
Performance: speed 60km/h (37mph); road range 480km (298 miles), 700km (434.8 miles) with long-range fuel tanks provided
Ground pressure: 0.83kg/cm² (11.87psi)
History: three types of separate loading ammunition were fired: APFSDS with a maximum range of 2,100m (1.3 miles); HEAT-FRAG with a maximum direct fire range of 4,000m (2.5 miles); and smoke with a maximum indirect range of 9,400m (5.8 miles). Its many variants included the T-72A baseline model, T-72B full-scale production model, T-72B(M) improved and the Czechoslovakian-produced T-74G.

The T-72A is one of the Soviets' most important current MBTs

T-64

Country of origin: USSR
Type: main battle tank
Production: the T-64 was first seen in 1970
Crew: three
Dimensions: length with gun forward 9.1m (29ft 10in); full length 6.4m (21ft); width overall 4.64m (15ft 2in) with skirts, 3.38m (11ft 1in) without skirts; height 2.4m (7ft 10in); ground clearance 0.377m (14.8in)
Armament system: one 125mm (4.92in) gun; one 7.62mm (0.31in) coaxial gun; one 12.7 (0.5in) AA gun
Armour: cast steel and composite, to a maximum thickness of 200mm (7.87in)
Powerplant: 5-cylinder opposed piston liquid-cooled diesel developing 700/750hp at 3,000rpm
Performance: speed 70km/h (43.5mph); road range 450km (279 miles), 700km (435 miles) with long-range fuel tanks fitted
Ground pressure: 1.09kg/cm² (15.58psi)
History: the long 125mm (4.92in) smoothbore gun fires APFSDS rounds to an estimated effective range of 2,000m (1.2 miles). The 12.7mm (0.5in) AA gun mounted on the commander's cupola can be fired automatically from inside the turret. Variants include F64A, T-64B, complete with laser rangefinder, and T-74-B-R.

The T-64B was the full production variant

T-62

Country of origin: USSR
Type: main battle tank
Production: introduced into service in 1962
Crew: four
Combat weight: 40,000kg (88,000lb) loaded
Dimensions: length including gun 9.335m (30ft 7in); width 3.3m (10ft 9in); height 2.395m (7ft 10in); ground clearance 0.425m (1ft 4in)
Armament system: one 115mm (4.55in) U-5TS, elevation +17°, depression −4°, 40 rounds carried; one 7.62mm (0.31in) PKT coaxial machine gun, 2,500 rounds carried
Armour: 20-170mm (0.8-6.43in) thick
Powerplant: Model V-12 water-cooled diesel engine developing 580hp at 2,000rpm
Performance: road speed 45.5km/h (28.26mph); road range 450km (279.5 miles); fuel 1,360 litres (299.56 Imp gal)
Ground pressure: 0.83kg/cm² (11.87psi)
History: a development of the T-54/T-55, the T-62, in addition to being longer, had a new turret and a new smooth-bore gun, capable of firing APFSDS with a muzzle velocity of 1,680m/sec (5,600ft/sec), HEAT with an MV of 1,000m/sec (3,333ft/sec) and two forms of HE fragmentation. Variants include the T-62A, the command model T-62K, the T-62M flamethrower, and an ARV designated M1977.

The initial model lacks the 12.7mm (0.5in) AA machine gun

T-55

Country of origin: USSR
Type: main battle tank
Production: first entered service in 1949
Crew: four
Dimensions: length with gun forward 9.02m (29ft 6in), full length 6.45m (21ft 2in); width overall 3.27m (10ft 8in); height 2.4m (7ft 9in); ground clearance 0.425m (1ft 4in)
Armament system: one 100mm (3.6in); one 7.62mm (0.31in) coaxial gun; one 7.62 (0.31in) bow machine gun; one 12.7mm (0.5in) AA machine gun (where fitted)
Armour: 20-203mm (0.79-8in) thick
Powerplant: Model V-55 V-12 water-cooled diesel engine developing 580hp at 2,000rpm
Performance: speed 50km/h (31.1mph); range 500km (310 miles)
Ground pressure: 0.8kg/cm² (11.44psi)
History: over 40,000 T-54s and T-55s have been built, and components have been used in the ZSU-23-4, ATS-59 and PTS. Unsophisticated, uncomfortable, cramped and often badly finished, the combination of a powerful gun, excellent range and cross-country potential made this MBT series very advanced when first produced. All models have an infrared driving light and searchlight, and an NBC system.

The T-55 utilised a more powerful engine than the T-54 on which it had been modelled

Vickers Defence Systems (ROF Leeds) FV 4030/4 Challenger

Country of origin: UK
Type: main battle tank
Production: began British service in 1983
Crew: four
Combat weight: 62 tonnes (136,000lb) laden
Dimensions: length with gun forward 11.55m (37ft 10in), with gun to rear 9.86m (32ft 4in); width overall 3.52m (11ft 6in), over tracks 3.42m (11ft 2in); height 2.88m (9ft 5in); ground clearance 0.5m (1ft 7in)
Armament system: 120mm (4.75in) L11 gun
Armour: steel and laminate
Powerplant: Rolls-Royce CV12 TCA 12-cylinder 60V direct injection 4-stroke diesel
Performance: speed up to approximately 60km/h (37.27mph)
Ground pressure: 0.9kg/cm² (12.87psi)
History: the Challenger's 120mm (4.75in) L11 semi-automatic gun fires bagged or combustible cased ammunition, loaded through a vertically-sliding breech and initiated by an electrically-primed vent tube. Up to 64 projectiles and 42 charge containers are carried. Secondary armament is provided by two 7.62mm (0.31in) machine guns, an L-8 coaxial machine gun and an L37 on the commander's cupola.

The Chobham armour cannot be manufactured in curved panels, hence the angular external appearance of the Challenger

Vickers Defence Systems (ROF Leeds) FV 4201 Chieftain Mk 1

Country of origin: UK

Type: main battle tank

Production: the Chieftain was first employed within BAOR in 1967

Crew: four

Combat weight: 55,000kg (121,000lb) loaded

Dimensions: length with gun forward 10.795m (35ft 4in), full length 7.52m (24ft 7in); width overall 3.66m (12ft); height 2.895 (9ft 5in); ground clearance 0.508m (1ft 7in)

Armament system: one 120mm (4.75in) L11 A2 gun; one 12.7mm (0.5in) ranging machine gun; one 7.62mm (0.31in) coaxial machine gun; one 7.62mm (0.31in) machine gun for AA defence

Armour: 150mm (5.9in)

Powerplant: Leyland L60 No 4 Mk 7A turbocharged inline multi-fuel engine developing 750bhp at 2,250rpm

Performance: road speed 48km/h (29.81mph); range 450km (279.5 miles)

Ground pressure: 0.9kg/cm² (12.87psi)

History: operated by a small joystick, and controllable either by the gunner or the commander, the main armament can be brought to bear, whether or not the tank is on the move, within a few seconds.

Numerically Britain's most important main battle tank

Vickers Defence Systems (ROF Leeds) FV 4201 Chieftain 900

Country of origin: UK
Type: main battle tank
Production: the first prototype was shown at the British Equipment Exhibition in 1982
Crew: four
Combat weight: 56,000kg (123,200lb)
Dimensions: length with gun forward 10.8m (36ft), 7.52m (25ft 8in) hull only; width 3.51m (11ft 8in); height 2.44m (8ft 1.5in) to turret top
Armament system: one 120mm (4.72in) L11As gun; one 7.62mm (0.31in) L8A2 coaxial machine gun; one 7.62mm (0.31in) L37A2 anti-aircraft and two quintuple smoke dischargers
Armour: Chobham laminate
Powerplant: Rolls-Royce 900E, 12-cylinder Condor, 60° direct injection turbocharged 4-stroke diesel engine developing 900bhp at 2,300rpm
Performance: speed 52km/h (32.3mph)
Ground pressure: 0.95kg/cm² (13.59psi)
History: based on the Chieftain chassis, the 900 has increased mobility and firepower. Main firepower is provided by the semi-automatic Royal Ordnance Factory 120mm (4.72in) rifled tank gun which is fitted with a fume-extractor. The 900 is comparable to the Chieftain 800 export variant.

The Chieftain 900 model offers better protection and a more powerful engine

ROF Leeds/ROF Woolwich/ Leyland/Vickers FV 4017 Centurion Mk 10

Country of origin: UK
Type: main battle tank
Production: developed by AEC Ltd in 1944
Crew: four
Combat weight: 51,820kg (114,004lb)
Dimensions: length with gun forward 9.854m (32ft 3in), full length 7.823m (25ft 7in); width overall 3.39m (11ft 1in); height 3.009m (9ft 10in); ground clearance 0.51m (1ft 8in)
Armament system: one 105mm (4.16in) tank gun; one 7.62mm (0.31in) coaxial machine gun; one 12.7mm (0.5in) ranging machine gun
Armour: cast and welded steel, varying in thickness between 17-152mm (0.66-6in)
Powerplant: Rolls-Royce Meteor Mk IV B 12-cylinder liquid-cooled petrol engine developing 650bhp at 2,550rpm
Performance: speed 34.6km/h (21.5mph); range 190km (118 miles)
Ground pressure: 0.95kg/cm² (13.59psi)
History: the Centurion first saw action in Korea and since then has distinguished itself throughout the world, particularly in the Israeli Army. The 105mm (4.16in) rifled tank gun is provided with a fume extractor on the barrel and has an effective range of 1,800m (1.14 miles) when using APDS round or 3,000-4,000m (1.86-2.48 miles) when using HESH.

ROF Leeds/ROF Woolwich/ Leyland/Vickers FV 4017 Upgraded Centurion

Country of origin: Israel
Type: main battle tank
Production: entered service in 1970
Crew: four
Combat weight: 51,820kg (114,243lb) loaded
Dimensions: length with gun forward 9.854m (32ft 4in), 7.823m (25ft 8in) hull only; width 3.39m (14ft 1in); height 3.009m (9ft 10in) to turret roof
Armament system: one 105mm (4.13in) L7-series rifled tank gun; one 12.7mm (0.5in) ranging machine gun, 600 rounds; two 7.62mm (0.31in) machine guns, coaxial and AA, 4,750 rounds; two 6-barrelled smoke dischargers
Armour: 17-152mm (0.67-6in)
Powerplant: Teledyne Continental AVDS-1790-2A diesel engine with automatic gearbox
Performance: road speed 43km/h (26.7mph); road range 380km (226 miles); fuel 1,037 litres (228 Imp gal)
Ground pressure: 0.95kg/cm² (13.58psi)
History: based on the original Centurion supplied to the Israeli Army in 1959. During the refits, the rear of the hull was enlarged, and elevated top decks were added to accommodate air vents. Finally, new fire-extinguishing and electrical systems were added.

Vickers Defence Systems (Vickers Valiant) Mk 7

Country of origin: UK
Type: main battle tank
Production: now ready for production
Crew: four
Combat weight: 43,600kg (95,920lb) loaded; 41,000kg (90,200lb) empty
Dimensions: length with gun forward 9.53m (31ft 3in), 7.51m (24ft 7in) hull only; width 3.3m (10ft 9in); height 2.64m (8ft 7in) to turret top, 3.24m (10ft 7in) to commander's sight; ground clearance 0.457m (1ft 6in)
Armament system: one 105mm (4.16in) gun, elevation +20°, depression −10°, 60 rounds carried; two 7.62mm (0.31in) machine guns, coaxial and AA, 3,000 rounds carried, and two 6-barrelled smoke dischargers
Armour: welded steel and appliqué laminate
Powerplant: General Motors 12V-71T 12-cylinder diesel engine developing 915bhp at 2,500rpm
Performance: road speed 59km/h (36.65mph); road range 603km (374.53 miles); fuel 1,000 litres (220.26 Imp gal)
Ground pressure: 0.81kg/cm² (11.58psi)
History: the hull is of welded aluminium. The Valiant is fitted with a Cendor commander day/night sight, a laser rangefinder, and a Marconi SFC 600 fire-control system.

Produced in association with Krauss-Maffei, using the Leopard 2's hull

58

Vickers Defence Systems Main Battle Tank Mk 3

Country of origin: UK, although under production in India
Type: main battle tank
Production: first delivered in 1965
Crew: four
Combat weight: 38,600kg (84,920lb) loaded; 36,000kg (79,200lb) empty
Dimensions: length with gun forward 9.788m (32ft 1in), full length 7.561m (24ft 9in); width overall 3.168m (10ft 4in); height 2.71m (8ft 10in); ground clearance 0.406m (1ft 3in)
Armament system: one 105mm (4.16in) tank gun; one 12.7mm (0.5in) ranging machine gun; one 7.62mm (0.31in) coaxial machine gun
Armour: welded steel, varying in thickness between 17-80mm (0.67-3.15in)
Powerplant: General Motors 12V 71T turbocharged diesel engine developing 800bhp at 2,500rpm
Performance: road speed 53km/h (32.92mph); range 600km (372.67 miles)
Ground pressure: 0.87kh/cm² (12.44psi)
History: Vickers MBTs have entered service in India under the name 'Vijayanta'. A six-barrelled smoke-discharger is mounted on both sides of the turret. The type is in service with Nigeria as the Eagle, and with Kenya. The Kuwaiti Mk 1s have been brought up to this standard.

The Mk 3 is an upgraded Mk 1, with
60 *Detroit Diesel engine*

General Dynamics M1 Abrams

Country of origin: USA
Type: main battle tank
Production: entered service in 1980
Crew: four
Combat weight: 54,432kg (119,750lb) loaded
Dimensions: length with gun forward 9.766m (32ft), 7.918m (25ft 11in) hull only; width overall 3.655m (11ft 11in); height 2.375m (7ft 9in) to turret roof, 2.895m (9ft 5in) overall; ground clearance 0.482m (1ft 6in) at centre hull, 0.432m (1ft 5in) at sides
Armament system: one 105mm (4.16in) tank gun; one 7.62 (0.31in) coaxial machine gun; one 12.7mm (0.5in) AA machine gun (commander) and one 7.62mm (0.3in) (loader)
Armour: steel and laminate
Powerplant: Avro Lycoming AGT-1500 gas turbine, developing 1,500hp at 3,000rpm
Performance: road speed 72.5km/h (45mph), 48.5km/h (30mph) across country
History: designed specifically for the European theatre. An advanced fire-control system for the fully-stabilised main armament is standard. Variants include the M1 Improved with additional armour, the M1A1, and more recently the M1A2, with automatic loader and thus reduced crew of three.

The successor to the M60 as the USA Army's MBT

General Dynamics M60

Country of origin: USA
Type: main battle tank
Production: the M60 entered service in 1959, being replaced by the M60A1 in 1962
Crew: four
Combat weight: 46,266kg (101,785lb) loaded, 42,184kg (92,805lb) empty
Dimensions: length with gun forward 9.309m (30ft 6in), 6.946m (22ft 9in) hull only; width overall 3.631m (11ft 10in); height 3.213m (10ft 6in); ground clearance 0.463m (1ft 6in)
Armament system: one 105mm (4.16in) tank gun; one 7.62mm (0.31in) coaxial gun; one 12.7mm (0.5in) AA machine gun
Armour: cast and welded steel
Powerplant: Continental AVDS-1790-2A 12-cylinder air-cooled diesel developing 750bhp at 2,400rpm
Performance: speed 48.3km/h (30mph); range 500km (310 miles)
Ground pressure: 0.783kg/cm² (11.2psi)
History: the main armament consists of the British 105mm (4.16mm) L7 gun, built under licence in the USA and designated the M68 gun. The turret is provided with an electro-hydraulic control system, with manual override, and is capable of a 360° traverse in 15 seconds, with maximum gun elevation of +20° and depression of −10°.

Chrysler (General Dynamics) M48

Country of origin: USA
Type: main battle tank
Production: first entered service in 1952
Crew: four
Combat weight: 44,906kg (98,793lb) loaded, 42,240kg (92,928lb) empty in early models; 47,173kg (103,781lb) loaded, 44,460kg (97,812lb) empty in later models
Dimensions: length with gun forward 8.687m (28ft 5in), 7.44m (24ft 4in) hull only; width overall 3.631m (11ft 10in); height 3.241m (10ft 7in) in early models, 3.086m (10ft 1in) in later models; ground clearance 0.393m (1ft 3in) in early models, 0.406m (1ft 3in) in later models
Armament system: one 90mm (3.56in) M41/L48 gun; one 7.62mm (0.3in) coaxial MG; one 12.7mm (0.5in) AA MG
Armour: welded and cast steel, varying in thickness between 12.74-120mm (0.5-4.72in)
Powerplant: AV-1790 5B/7/7B/7C Continental air-cooled engine developing 750hp at 2,400rpm; later models fit AVDS-1790-2A/D Continental developing 750hp at 2,400rpm
Performance: speed 48km/h (29.81mph); range 400km (248.45 miles), models vary
Ground pressure: 0.83kg/cm² (11.87psi)
History: the M48 replaced the M47 and has evolved through many variants and modifications.

Detroit Tank Plant/American Automotive M47

Country of origin: USA
Type: medium tank
Production: entered service with USA Army in 1953
Crew: five
Combat weight: 44,707kg (98,355lb) loaded, 42,130kg (92,686lb) empty
Dimensions: length with gun forward 8.553m (28ft), 6.307m (20ft) hull only; width overall 3.51m (11ft 6in); height 3.016m (9ft 1in) to commander's cupola; ground clearance 0.469m (1ft 6in)
Armament system: one 90mm (3.56in) M36 gun, one 7.62mm (0.31in) coaxial gun; one 12.7mm (0.5in) AA machine gun in the bow
Armour: welded steel, varying in thickness between 12.7-102mm (0.5-4in)
Powerplant: Continental Model AV-1790-5B, 7 or 7B, V-12, 4-cycle, air-cooled petrol engine developing 810bhp at 2,800rpm
Performance: speed 48km/h (29.81mph); range 128km (79.5 miles)
Ground pressure: 0.935kg/cm² (13.37psi)
History: some 8,676 units of the M47 were built, mostly for export under the United States Mutual Aid Program. The main armament consists of the M36 90mm (3.56in) rifled gun, with either a T-shaped or cylindrical blast deflector.

Now obsolete in relation to the modern battlefield

M4A1 Sherman

Country of origin: USA
Type: medium tank
Production: introduced in October 1941
Crew: five
Combat weight: 32,044kg (70,497lb) loaded
Dimensions: length 7.39m (24ft 2in); width 2.717m (8ft 10in); height 3.425m (11ft 2in); ground clearance 0.43m (1ft 5in)
Armament system: one 76mm (3in) gun, elevation +25°, depression −10°, 71 rounds carried; two 7.62mm (0.31in) machine guns, coaxial and bow, 6,250 rounds carried; one 12.7mm (0.5in) AA machine gun, 600 rounds carried
Armour: 12-75mm (0.48-2.97in)
Powerplant: R-975-C4, developing 400bhp at 2,400rpm
Performance: road speed 39km/h (24mph); range 160km (99.38 miles) cruising; fuel 651 litres (143.39 Imp gal)
Ground pressure: 1.02kg/cm² (14.59psi)
History: the most famous Allied tank of World War II, the M4 Sherman remains in service, despite its age. Many of the Sherman 'gun-tanks' have now been further modified into self-propelled mortars, armoured ambulances, and engineer vehicles.

An M51 Super Sherman with gun traversed to the rear

Type 62

Country of origin: China
Type: light tank
Crew: four
Combat weight: 18,000kg (39,600lb) loaded
Dimensions: length with gun forward 8.27m (27ft 1in), 6.91m (22ft 7in) hull only; width 3.25m (10ft 7in); height 2.19m (7ft 2in) to turret roof; ground clearance 0.37m (1ft 2.5in)
Armament system: one 85mm (3.37in) gun, elevation $+18°$, depression $-5°$; one 7.62mm (0.31in) coaxial machine gun; one 12.7mm (0.5in) AA machine gun
Armour: 14mm (0.55in)
Powerplant: V-12 diesel engine developing 520hp at 2,000rpm
Performance: road speed 50km/h (31.06mph); range 300km (186.34 miles); fuel 545 litres (120 Imp gal)
History: a very basic light tank, intended for operations in adverse terrain, it lacks an NBC system, amphibious capability and night vision devices.

The Type 62 is little more than a scaled-down version of the Type 59

72 *MBT shown* opposite

Creusot-Loire AMX-13

Country of origin: France
Type: light tank
Production: entered service 1953
Crew: three
Combat weight: 15,000kg (33,000lb) loaded; 13,000kg (28,600lb) empty
Dimensions: length with gun forward 6.38m (20ft 11in), 4.88m (16ft) hull only; width overall 2.5m (8ft 2in); height 2.3m (7ft 6in); ground clearance 0.37m (1ft 2in)
Armament system: one 90mm (3.56in) gun; one 7.62mm (0.31in) coaxial gun
Powerplant: SOFAM Model 8 GX6 8-cylinder water-cooled petrol engine developing 250hp at 3,200rpm
Performance: speed 60km/h (37.27mph); range 350-400km (217-248 miles)
Ground pressure: 0.76kg/cm² (10.87psi)
History: over 4,000 have been built, in addition to several thousand adaptations. These include 105mm (4.13in) and 155mm (6.1in) self-propelled guns, armoured personnel carriers, and anti-aircraft vehicles, which make the AMX-13 the most successful light tank in the world.

The world's most successful light tank, the AMX-13/90 is an upgraded version

PT-76

Country of origin: USSR
Type: light tank
Production: the PT-76 entered service in the Soviet Union in 1952
Crew: three
Combat weight: 14,000kg (30,800lb) loaded
Dimensions: length with gun forward 7.625mm (25ft), 6.91m (22ft 7in) hull only; width overall 3.16m (10ft 4in); height 2.2m (7ft 2in); ground clearance 0.37m (1ft 2in)
Armament system: one 76.2mm (3.1in) D-56 gun; one 7.62mm (0.31in) SGMT coaxial machine gun
Armour: welded steel varying in thickness between 5-17mm (0.2-0.67in)
Powerplant: Model V6 6-cylinder inline water-cooled diesel engine developing 240hp at 1,800rpm
Performance: road speed 44km/h (27.33mph), over water 11km/h (6.83mph); range 255km (158.39 miles)
Ground pressure: 0.48kg/cm² (6.86psi)
History: the PT-76 has no NBC or night-vision equipment. It has seen service in both the Middle and Far East, but is vulnerable against more modern armament and has now been replaced as a front-line reconnaissance vehicle by the BMP.

The PT-76 light tanks had a primary amphibious role

Cadillac (General Motors) M41

Country of origin: USA
Type: light tank
Production: the M41 entered service in 1951
Crew: four
Combat weight: 23,495kg (51,689lb) loaded
Dimensions: length with gun forward 8.212m (26ft 11in), 5.819m (19ft 1in) excluding gun; width 3.198m (10ft 5in); height 3.075m (10ft 1in) with machine gun, 2.726m (8ft 11in) without; ground clearance 0.45m (1ft 5.5in)
Armament system: one 76mm (3.1in) M32 gun, elevation +19°, depression −10°, 57 rounds carried; one 7.62mm (0.31in) M1919A4E1 coaxial MG, 5,000 rounds; one 12.7mm (0.5in) M2 A, 2,175 rounds
Armour: 12-38mm (0.48-1.5in)
Powerplant: M41 and M41A1 Continental or Lycoming AOS-895-5, M41A2 and M41A3, Continental or Lycoming 1051-895-5 6-cylinder air-cooled supercharged petrol engine developing 500hp at 2,800rpm
Performance: road speed 72km/h (44.72mph); range 161km (100 miles); fuel 530 litres (116.74 Imp gal)
Ground pressure: 0.72kg/cm² (10.3psi)
History: for many years the standard reconnaissance vehicle of United States armoured regiments, replacing the earlier M24 Chaffee.

The M41 is now outdated and obsolescent

M551 General Sheridan

Country of origin: USA
Type: light tank/reconnaissance vehicle
Crew: four
Combat weight: 15,830kg (34,826lb) loaded; 13,589kg (29,896lb) empty
Dimensions: length 6.299m (20ft 7in); width 2.819m (9ft 2in); height including MG 2.946m (9ft 7in); ground clearance 0.48m (1ft 7in)
Armament system: one 152mm (6.02in) M81 launcher, elevation +19.5°, depression −8°, 20 conventional rounds and 10 Shillelagh missiles carried; one 7.62mm (0.31in) M73 coaxial machine gun, 3,080 rounds carried; one 12.7mm (0.5in) M2 machine gun at commander's cupola, 1,000 rounds carried; eight grenade launchers, four on each side of turret
Powerplant: Detroit Diesel 6V53T developing 300hp at 2,800rpm
Performance: road speed 70km/h (43.48mph); road range 600km (372.67 miles); fuel 598 litres (131.72 Imp gal)
Ground pressure: 0.49kg/cm² (7.01psi)
History: the first prototype was completed in 1962, designated XM551. The first production vehicle was completed in 1966; since then, some 1,700 were produced until production halted in 1970. The M551 replaced the M41 with the USA Army.

The launcher has a range of 3,000m (1.86 miles)

Cadillac (General Motors) M24 Chaffee

Country of origin: USA
Type: light tank
Production: first delivered in 1944
Crew: four or five
Combat weight: 18,370kg (40,414lb) loaded; 16,440kg (36,168lb) empty
Dimensions: length including gun 5.486m (17ft 11in); width 2.95m (9ft 8in); height 2.77m (9ft 1in) including machine gun, 2.46m (8ft) to cupola; ground clearance 0.457m (1ft 6in)
Armament system: one 75mm (2.97in) M6 gun, elevation +15°, depression −10°, 48 rounds carried; one 12.7mm (0.5in) M2 AA machine gun, 440 rounds carried; two 7.62mm (0.31in) machine guns, coaxial and bow
Armour: 10-38mm (0.4-1.5in)
Powerplant: two Cadillac Model 44T24 petrol V-8 water-cooled engines each developing 110hp at 3,400rpm
Performance: road speed 55km/h (34.16mph); road range 281km (174.53 miles); fuel 416 litres (91.63 Imp gal)
Ground pressure: 0.78kg/cm² (11.15psi)
History: the M24 Chaffee saw action in the final stages of World War II, but is no longer in service in its original form. Noted for its speed and manoeuvrability, the M24 held up the North Korean invasion of the South in 1950.

The M24 Chaffee replaced the M3
82 *and M5 series*

ENGESA EE-9 Cascavel

Country of origin: Brazil
Type: armoured car
Production: available in 1974
Crew: three
Combat weight: 12,200kg (26,840lb) loaded; 11,800kg (25,960lb) empty
Dimensions: length with gun forward 6.22m (20ft 4in), 5.19m (17ft) hull only; width 2.59m (8ft 5in); height 2.36m (7ft 8in) to cupola; ground clearance 0.375m (1ft 2.75in)
Armament system: one 90mm (3.56in) gun, elevation +15°, depression −8°, 45 rounds carried; two 7.62mm (0.31in) machine guns, one coaxial and one optional AA, 2,400 rounds
Armour: 12mm (0.48in) maximum
Powerplant: Mercedes-Benz OM-352A 6-cylinder water-cooled turbocharged diesel developing 190hp at 2,800rpm
Performance: speed 100km/h (62.11mph); range 1,000km (621.12 miles); fuel 360 litres (79.3 Imp gal)
History: the EE-9 has many automotive components in common with an EE-11 Urutu APC. Variants include the Mk I initial production variant; Mk II export model fitted with a French H-90 turret; Mk III fitted with an ENGESA ET-90 turret; Mk IV and Mk V, each improved models with different powerplants.

The series runs from Mk I through to Mk V with upgrades

ENGESA EE-3 Jararaca

Country of origin: Brazil
Type: scout car
Production: began 1980
Crew: three
Combat weight: 5,200kg (11,440lb) maximum
Dimensions: length 4.195m (13ft 9in); width 2.13m (6ft 11in); height without armament 1.56m (5ft 1in); ground clearance 0.315m (1ft 0.5in)
Armament system: one 12.7mm (0.5in) machine gun
Armour: hull consists of an outer layer of hard steel and an inner layer of softer steel roll-bonded and heat-treated for maximum protection
Powerplant: Daimler-Benz OM-314 4-cylinder water-cooled diesel engine developing 120hp at 2.800rpm
Performance: speed 90km/h (56mph); range 750km (466 miles); fuel 135 litres (30 Imp gal)
History: can be fitted with a wide range of armament including a 7.62mm (0.31in) or 12.7mm (0.5in) machine gun, a 20mm (0.8in) cannon, a 60mm (2.4in) breech-loaded mortar, a 106mm (4.16in) M40 recoilless gun, or a MILAN ATGW.

A light scout car with good cross-country mobility

GIAT AMX-10RC

Country of origin: France
Type: reconnaissance vehicle
Production: entered service in 1979
Crew: four
Dimensions: length 6.35m (20ft 9in); width 2.86m (9ft 4in); height 2.68m (8ft 9in)
Armament system: one 105mm (4.16in) gun; one 7.62mm (0.31in) CA; two double smoke dischargers
Armour: welded aluminium
Powerplant: Hispano-Suiza HS-115 8-cylinder supercharged diesel developing 280hp at 3,000rpm
Performance: road speed 85km/h (52.8mph), 7km/h (4.35mph) over water; range 800km (496.89 miles)
History: designed for anti-tank combat, it is amphibious without preparation, and has very good mobility. The 105mm (4.16in) gun fires a high-velocity hollow-charged shell, and is targeted by a high-performance fire-control system, with a ×10 magnification laser range-finder and automatic fire-correction control, fitted with a low-light TV for night operation. The AMX-10RAC is available with TS 90 turret and two other variants are proposed.

This excellent vehicle is basically the reconnaissance version of the AMX-10P

Panhard EBR

Country of origin: France
Type: wheeled armoured car
Production: began 1950; ended 1960
Crew: four
Combat weight: 13,500kg (29,700lb) loaded
Dimensions: length 6.15m (20ft 2in) including FL-11 turret, 5.56m (18ft 2in) vehicle only; width 2.42m (7ft 11in); height 2.24m (7ft 4in) with FL-11 on four wheels; ground clearance 0.33m (1ft 1in) on four wheels
Armament system: one 75mm (2.97in) gun, elevation +15°, depression −10°, 56 rounds carried; one 7.5mm (0.3in) coaxial machine gun
Armour: 10-40mm (0.4-1.58in)
Powerplant: one 150kW (201hp) Panhard 12H 6000 petrol engine driving a 4 × 4 (optional 8 × 8) layout
Performance: road speed 105km/h (65.22mph); range 650km (403.73 miles); fuel 380 litres (84 Imp gal)
Ground pressure: 0.75kg/cm² (10.73psi) on eight wheels
History: the four-man crew consisted of commander, gunner and two drivers. The EBR was fitted with an FL-11; the ERB ETT armoured personnel carrier version was lighter at 13,000kg (26,660lb), carrying a crew of three and 12 infantry.

The EBR 75 and EBR 90 are both still in limited service in North Africa

Renault VBC 90

Country of origin: France
Type: armoured car
Crew: three
Combat weight: 13,500kg (29,762lb)
Dimensions: length 5.495m (18ft); width 2.49m (8ft 2in); height 2.55m (8ft 4in)
Armament system: one 90mm (3.56in) gun; one 7.62mm (0.31in) CA, and one 7.62mm (0.31in) AP
Armour: cast and welded steel
Powerplant: one 170kW (228hp) Renault VI MIDS 06-20-45 diesel engine driving a 6 × 6 layout
Performance: road speed 92km/h (57.2mph); road range 1,000km (621 miles); fording 1.2m (3.9ft); gradient 50%; side slope 30%; vertical obstacle 0.6m (1.96ft); trench 1m (3.25ft); ground clearance not revealed; fuel not revealed
History: this powerful yet highly mobile six-wheeled anti-tank armoured fighting vehicle's GIAT 7S 90 turret houses an accurate high-performance 90mm (3.56in) gun firing APFSDS, hollow-charge and HE ammunition, with a range of 1,700m (1.05 miles). The gun has an effective time-control system, linked with a SOPTAC computer.

The VBC 90 is an armoured car with an exceptionally powerful gun

Panhard AML H90

Country of origin: France
Type: light wheeled armoured car
Production: entered service in 1961
Crew: three
Combat weight: 5.5 tonnes (12,100lb)
Dimensions: length 3.79m (12ft 5in); width 1.97m (6ft 5in); height 2.07m (6ft 9in)
Armament system: one 90mm (3.56in) and one 7.62mm (0.31in) CA; two smoke dischargers on both sides of the turret
Armour: 8-12mm (0.32-0.47in) welded steel
Powerplant: Panhard Model 4 HD 4-cylinder air-cooled petrol engine developing 90hp at 4,700rpm
Performance: road speed 90km/h (55.9mph); range 600km (372.67 miles)
History: the AML H90 is produced for both home and export markets in large quantities, fitted with a powerfully armed Hispano-Suiza turret. The AML Lynx 90 variant is the current production model and has an improved turret. The AML HE 60-7 turret has twin 7.62mm (0.31in) machine guns and a 60mm (2.36in) HB-60 mortar; other variants are the AML 20, AML Eclairage scout car and the South African licence-built Eland Mk 1 (originally) and currently Mk 7 or Eland 90.

A four-wheel drive armoured car with powerful gun, mounted on a
Hispano-Suiza turret

Panhard ERC 90 F4 Sagaie 2

Country of origin: France
Type: wheeled armoured car
Crew: three
Combat weight: 10,000kg (22,046lb)
Dimensions: length with gun forward 7.97m (26.15ft), 5.57m (18.27ft) hull only; width 2.7m (8.86ft); height 2.3m (7.55ft)
Armament system: one 90mm (3.54in) GIAT CS Super (F4) rifled gun; two 7.62mm (0.31in) machine guns and two or four smoke dischargers on each side of the turret; the turret is electrically powered, and the main gun lacks stabilisation in either elevation +15° to −8° or azimuth (306°); an optical fire-control system is fitted
Armour: welded steel
Powerplant: two 75kW (101hp) Peugeot XD 34T diesel engines or two 108kW (145hp) Peugeot PVR petrol engines driving a 4 × 4 (optional 6 × 6) layout
Performance: road speed 110km/h (68.4mph), 7.2km/h (4.5mph) over water, driven by two water jets; road range 600km (373 miles); ground clearance 0.35m (1.15ft); fuel 350 litres (77 Imp gal)

An improved version of the Sagaie 1, with an uparmoured SAMM TTB 90 turret in place of the Sagaie 1's TS 90 type

Thyssen Henschel Spahpanzer Luchs

Country of origin: West Germany
Type: wheeled armoured reconnaissance vehicle
Production: entered service in 1975
Crew: four
Combat weight: 19.5 tonnes (42,900lb)
Dimensions: length 7.743m (25ft 4in); width 2.98m (9ft 9in); height 2.9m (9ft 6in)
Armament system: one 20mm (0.8in) cannon and one 7.62mm (0.31in) machine gun
Armour: welded steel
Powerplant: Daimler-Benz 10-cylinder 390hp water-cooled multi-fuel engine
Performance: speed 90km/h (55.9mph); range 800km (496.89 miles)
History: a replacement for the Bundeswehr's ageing M41s and Hotchkiss SPz 11-2 reconnaissance vehicles. The Spahpanzer Luchs is the German Army's standard amphibian reconnaissance vehicle. It is highly mobile, having eight-wheel steering when required off-road, four-wheel steering being normally employed. The type has a full NBC system and passive night vision devices.

The German Army's standard
amphibious reconnaissance vehicle

IVECO/Fiat/OTO Melara Tipo 6616

Country of origin: Italy
Type: armoured car
Production: entered service in 1977
Crew: three
Combat weight: 7,400kg (16,280lb) loaded; 6,900kg (15,180lb) empty
Dimensions: length 5.37mm (17ft 7in); width 2.5m (8ft 2in); height 2.035m (6ft 8in) to top of turret
Armament system: one 20mm (0.8in) Rh. 202 cannon, elevation +35°, depression −5°, 400 rounds carried; one 7.62mm (0.31in) coaxial machine gun, 1,000 rounds carried; two triple smoke dischargers on both sides of the turret
Armour: 6-8mm (0.24-0.32in) welded steel
Powerplant: Model 8062.24 supercharged inline diesel developing 160hp at 3,200rpm
Performance: road speed 100km/h (62.11mph); 5km/h (3.11mph) over water; range 700km (434.78 miles); fuel 150 litres (33.04 gal)
History: a private venture project by Fiat and OTO Melara, the Type 6616 is used in limited numbers in primary roles on the domestic front.

BRDM-2

Country of origin: USSR
Type: armoured reconnaissance vehicle
Production: entered service in 1966
Crew: two + four, depending on variant
Combat weight: 7 tonnes (15,400lb)
Dimensions: length 5.75m (18ft 10in); height 2.31m (7ft 6in); width 2.35m (7ft 8in)
Armament system: 14.5mm (0.57in) machine gun and 7.62mm (0.31) machine gun
Armour: 10mm (0.4in)
Powerplant: GAZ-41 V-8 water-cooled petrol engine developing 140hp at 3,400rpm
Performance: road speed 100km/h (62.11mph), 10km/h (6.21mph) over water; range 750km (465.84 miles)
History: the BRDM-2 represents a considerable advance over its predecessor, the BRDM-1. The rear-mounted engine has greater speed and range; it has slightly improved ground clearance and a reasonable defensive armament and amphibious capability, and is also fitted with IR night-driving equipment. In the anti-tank role, the turret is removed; in the SAGGER variant there is a flat one-piece cover. The BRDM-2 is also used as the basis for the SA-9 GASKIN SAM system, and there is a chemical reconnaissance version, the BRDM-2 RkH.

The BRDM-2 has a more powerful engine than the BRDM-1, and it also has enclosed armament

BRDM-1

Country of origin: USSR
Type: armoured reconnaissance vehicle
Production: entered service in 1959
Crew: two + three, depending on variant
Combat weight: 5.6 tonnes (12,320lb)
Dimensions: length 5.7m (18ft 8in); width 2.25m (7ft 4in); height 1.9m (6ft 2in)
Armament system: 7.62mm (0.31in) machine gun
Armour: 10mm (0.4in)
Powerplant: GAZ-40P 6-cylinder water-cooled petrol engine developing 90hp at 3,400rpm
Performance: road speed 80km/h (49.69mph), 9km/h (5.59mph) over water; range 500km (310.56 miles)
History: the BRDM (Bronevaya Rasvedyvakei-naya Dosernaya Maschina) armoured recon-naissance vehicle was relatively fast, possessed good cross-country performance owing to the tyre pressurisation system and retractable belly wheels, and most importantly, it was amphi-bious. The only preparation required was to raise the bow trim blade and to open the rear cover of the water-jet unit.

Far inferior to the BRDM-2, the BRDM-1 became standard in Warsaw Pact armies in about 1960

Alvis FV 601 (C) Saladin Mk 2

Country of origin: UK
Type: armoured car
Production: entered service in 1959 and remained in production until 1972
Crew: three
Combat weight: 11.59 tonnes (25,498lb)
Dimensions: length 5.284m (17ft 3in), 4.93m (16ft 2in) hull only; width 2.54m (8ft 3in); height 2.19m (7ft 2in)
Armament system: 76mm (3in) gun; 7.62mm (0.31in) coaxial machine gun
Armour: 8.3mm (0.32in)
Powerplant: Rolls-Royce B.80 Mk 6A 8-cylinder petrol engine developing 170hp at 3,750rpm
Performance: speed 72km/h (44.72mph); range 400km (248.45 miles)
History: still in widespread use in African and Middle Eastern countries. The 6 × 6 chassis, which is common to the Saracen APC and Stalwart high-mobility load carrier, provides a fast and versatile platform for the powerful ROF 76mm (3in) gun. The vehicle's mobility was enhanced by fitting run-flat tyres, and it has a capacity to keep moving despite the loss of several wheels.

Still in use, though now outdated, especially lacking night-vision equipment

Alvis FV 101 Scorpion

Country of origin: UK
Type: combat vehicle reconnaissance (tracked)
Production: entered service in 1972
Crew: three
Combat weight: 8,000kg (17,600lb) loaded
Dimensions: length 4.794m (15ft 8in); width 2.235m (7ft 3in); height 2.102m (6ft 10in)
Armament system: one 76mm (3in) gun, elevation +35°, depression −10°, 40 rounds carried; one 7.62mm (0.31in) machine gun, 3,000 rounds carried; two 4-barrelled smoke dischargers
Powerplant: Jaguar 6-cylinder water-cooled petrol engine developing190bhp at 4,750rpm
Performance: road speed 80.5km/h (50mph); range 644km (400 miles); fuel 423 litres (93.17 Imp gal)
Ground pressure: 0.36kg/cm² (5.15psi)
History: the Scorpion vehicle, properly described, is a scouting vehicle, the 76mm (3in) gun being used to 'get the vehicle out of trouble' rather than to engage in offensive action. It is used with a mix of other CVRT family types, including the 30mm (1.18in) Rarden cannon-equipped 'Scimitar'. The Scorpion 90 variant has been updated in an improved variant for Malaysia.

An extensive family of models, derived from the Spartan armoured
personnel carrier

ROF Leeds FV 721 Fox

Country of origin: UK
Type: combat vehicle reconnaissance (wheeled)
Production: entered service in 1973
Crew: three
Combat weight: 6,356kg (13,983lb) loaded; 5,174kg (11,383lb) empty
Dimensions: length 4.22m (13ft 10in); width 2.13m (6ft 11in); height 2.2m (7ft 2in)
Armament system: 30mm (1.18in) Rarden cannon effective against APVs to 1,000m (3,279ft); 7.62m (0.31in) GPMG
Armour: welded aluminium
Powerplant: Jaguar XK 4.2 militarised 6-cylinder engine developing 190hp at 5,000rpm
Performance: speed 104km/h (64.6mph), 5km/h (3.12mph) over water; road range 434km (269 miles); fuel 145 litres (32.22 Imp gal)
Ground pressure: 0.46kg/cm² (6.57psi)
History: the logical successor to the Ferret, the Fox is equipped with day and night sighting plus the battle-proven Rarden 30mm (1.18in). Storage allows up to 99 rounds of 30mm (1.18in) and 2,600 rounds of 7.62mm (0.31in) to be carried. Light alloy armour gives protection against heavy machine gun fire and artillery splinters. The Fox is truly air-portable, and it is possible to parachute two together, on a special pallet.

An all-aluminium light armoured
car, derived from the Ferret

Daimler FV 711F Ferret Mk 4

Country of origin: UK
Type: light scout car
Production: began 1952; ceased 1971
Crew: two or three
Combat weight: 5,400kg (11,880lb) loaded; 4,725kg (10,395lb) empty
Dimensions: length 4.095m (13ft 8in); width 2.13m (7ft 1in); height 2.336m (7ft 11in); ground clearance 0.43m (1ft 4.9in)
Armament system: 30mm (1.18in) Browning machine gun
Armour: welded steel varying in thickness between 8-16mm (0.315-0.63in)
Powerplant: Rolls-Royce B60 Mk 6A 6-cylinder water-cooled petrol engine developing 129bhp at 3,750rpm
Performance: speed 80km/h (49.69mph), 3.8km/h (2.36mph) over water; road range 300km (186 miles); fuel 96 litres (21 Imp gal)
History: one of the most widely distributed liaison/reconnaissance/IS patrol vehicles in the world. The original Mk 1 was highly mobile, and with a very low silhouette. The armament was an optical Bren gun on a pintle mount. The Mk 2 was fitted with a light, manually operated turret, mounting a 30mm (1.18in) Browning machine gun.

The Mk 4 is an upgraded version, with stronger suspension and a folded flotation screen

Short Brothers Shorland S51 Mk 3

Country of origin: UK
Type: armoured patrol car (wheeled)
Production: entered service in 1965
Crew: three
Combat weight: 3.36 tonnes (7,392lb) loaded; 2.93 tonnes (6,460lb) empty
Dimensions: length 4.59m (15ft); width 1.77m (5ft 9in); height 2.28m (7ft 5in)
Armament system: one 7.62mm (0.31in) machine gun, 1,500 rounds carried; two 4-barrel smoke dischargers (optional)
Armour: 8.25-11mm (0.32-0.43in)
Powerplant: Rover 6-cylinder petrol engine developing 91bhp at 4,500rpm
Performance: road speed 88.5km/h (55.31mph); range 257km (160.6 miles) with standard tank, 514km (321.25 miles) with long-range tank; fuel 64 litres (14.08 Imp gal) standard and 128 litres (28.17 Imp gal) long-range
Ground pressure: 2.4kg/cm² (34.2psi)
History: the Landrover, in various forms, is in service with a considerable number of police and armed forces throughout the world. The first Shorland armoured patrol car was based on a standard 2.750m (12ft 1in) LWB Landrover, with armoured bodywork by Short Brothers and Harland, of Belfast.

Designed for use by security forces rather than the military

Cadillac Gage Commando Scout

Country of origin: USA
Type: wheeled scout/reconnaissance vehicle
Production: entered service in 1983
Crew: one + one or one + two
Combat weight: 6,577kg (14,469lb)
Dimensions: length 4.699m (15ft 4in); width 2.057m (6ft 8in); height 2.235m (7ft 3in)
Armament system: two 7.62mm (0.31in) machine guns
Armour: welded steel
Powerplant: Cummins V-6 diesel engine developing 149hp at 3,300rpm
Performance: speed 88.5km/h (54.97mph); range 800km (496.89 miles); fuel 208 litres (45.81 Imp gal)
History: various armaments can be fitted, including twin 7.62mm (0.31in) machine guns with 1,600 rounds ammunition, or one 7.62mm (0.31in) and one 12.7mm (0.5in) machine gun, or twin 12.7mm (0.5in) machine guns. A 20mm (0.79in) or 30mm (1.18in) cannon can also be fitted.

The Commando Scout is a useful light reconnaissance vehicle, which

first entered service with Indonesia

Stehr Saurer 4K 4FA

Country of origin: Austria
Type: armoured personnel carrier
Production: began 1961; ended 1969
Crew: two + eight
Combat weight: 15,000kg (33,000lb) loaded
Dimensions: length 5.4m (17ft 8in); width 2.5m (8ft 2in); height 2.17m (7ft 1in) including turret; ground clearance 0.42m (1ft 4.5in)
Armament system: one 20mm (0.8in) Oerlikon cannon with an elevation of +70° and a depression of −12°
Armour: welded steel varying in thickness between 8-35mm (0.315-1.38in)
Powerplant: Steyr Model 4FA 6-cylinder diesel engine developing 250hp at 2,400rpm
Performance: road speed 65km/h (40.37mph); range 370km (229.81 miles); fuel 184 litres (40.53 Imp gal)
Ground pressure: 0.52kg/cm² (7.44psi)
History: the main production model of a successful APC series. The design was recast with a different hull shape after the first prototype and entered production as the 4K4F, followed by the 4K3FA, with a more powerful engine. The type has been developed as the basis of a self-propelled rocket-launcher carrying two nine-tube banks for 81mm (3.2in) SNORA rockets.

This is a large family of armoured personnel carriers with many options available

Beherman Demoen BDX

Country of origin: Belgium/Eire/UK
Type: armoured personnel carrier (wheeled)
Production: entered service in 1978
Crew: two + 10
Combat weight: 10.7 tonnes (23,540lb)
Dimensions: length 5.05m (16ft 6in); width 2.5m (8ft 2in); height 2.84m (9ft 3in) with turret, 2.06m (6ft 9in) without
Armament system: varies
Armour: welded steel varying in thickness between 9.5-12.7mm (0.37- 0.5in)
Powerplant: Chrysler V-8 180bhp petrol engine
Performance: speed 100km/h (62.11mph); range 500-900km (310.56-559 miles)
History: the original vehicle was a basic wheeled APC affording a high degree of ballistic protection, making it particularly suited to the police/internal security role. A variety of weapon fits is available, including 7.62mm (0.31in) and 12.7mm (0.5in) machine-gun turrets, 20mm (0.8in) cannon and anti-tank missiles, and 81mm (3.2in) mortars.

Improved and upgraded variant of
the Timoney Mk 5

ACEC Cobra

Country of origin: Belgium
Type: armoured personnel carrier
Crew: three + nine
Combat weight: 7,500kg (16,500lb) loaded
Dimensions: length 4.2m (13ft 9in); width 2.7m (8ft 10in); height 1.65m (5ft 4in) to hull top; ground clearance 0.4m (1ft 3.75in)
Armament system: one 12.7mm (0.5in) machine gun; two 101mm (4in) rocket launchers; two 7.62mm (0.31in) bow machine guns; two triple rifle grenade launchers
Armour: welded steel
Powerplant: one 142kW (190hp) Cummins VT-190 diesel engine developing 143hp at 3,300rpm
Performance: road speed 80km/h (49.69mph), 7km/h (4.35mph) over water; range 600km (372.67 miles); fuel 309 litres (68 Imp gal)
Ground pressure: 0.29kg/cm² (4.15psi)
History: the crew comprises two drivers at the front, each operating a bow-mounted 7.62mm (0.31in) machine gun, and a gunner/vehicle commander. There is a large door at the rear for the infantry to enter, but no facility for them to fire small arms once inside. Fully amphibious, the Cobra is propelled in the water by its tracks.

The Cobra utilises an unusual
diesel-electric drive

ENGESA EE-11 Urutu

Country of origin: Brazil
Type: armoured personnel carrier
Production: entered service in 1975
Crew: 14
Combat weight: 13,000kg (28,600lb) loaded; 11,000kg (24,200lb) empty
Dimensions: length 6m (19ft 8in); width 2.6m (8ft 6in); height 2.72m (8ft 11in) to top of machine-gun mount, 0.9m (6ft 10in) to hull top
Armament system: 60mm (2.36in) breech-loaded Brandt mortar
Armour: maximum 12mm (0.48in)
Powerplant: Mercedes-Benz OM-32A 6-cylinder water-cooled turbocharged diesel engine developing 190hp at 2,800rpm
Performance: road speed 90km/h (55.9mph); 8km/h (4.97mph) over water; range 1,000km (621.12 miles); fuel 380 litres (83.7 Imp gal)
History: designed to meet the operational requirements of the Brazilian Army, with a wide range of armament installation options, from simple pintle-mounted machine-gun mounts to the tank-destroyer version equipped with a 90mm (3.54in) gun. This very cost-effective vehicle is in service with many South American countries and Libya.

Produced with a great deal of commonality with the EE-9, the Urutu is offered with a variety of powerplants

124

OT-64

Country of origin: Czechoslovakia
Type: armoured personnel carrier (wheeled)
Crew: two + 14
Combat weight: 14.4tonnes (31,680lb)
Dimensions: length 7.44m (24ft 4in); width 2.5m (8ft 2in); height 2.71m (8ft 10in) including turret, 2.3m (7ft 6in) without
Armament system: various machine guns, depending on model
Powerplant: Tatra T 928-14 V-8 diesel engine developing 180hp at 2,000rpm
Performance: speed 95km/h (59mph), 9km/h (5.59mph) over water; range 650km (403.73 miles)
History: the OT series of APCs was developed by Czechoslovakia in preference to the USSR BTR-60 and entered Czech and Polish service in 1964. The original model OT-64A was an armoured carrier based on the Tatra 813 8 × 8 truck, and featured no additional armament except for the troops' personal weapons. The OT-64B has an open turret with either a 7.62mm (0.31in) machine gun or 12.7 (0.5in) machine gun.

The OT-64 has finally been replaced by the Polish Army

OT-62/TOPAS

Country of origin: Czechoslovakia
Type: armoured personnel carrier (tracked)
Crew: two + 14
Combat weight: 16.4 tonnes (36,080lb)
Dimensions: length 7m (22ft 11in); width 3.14m (10ft 3in); height 2.1m (6ft 10in)
Armament system: depends on model
Armour: 10-14mm (0.4-0.55in)
Powerplant: Model PV-6 6-cylinder inline diesel developing 300hp at 1,800rpm
Performance: speed 60km/h (37.27mph), 11km/h (6.83mph) over water; range 350-570km (217-354 miles), depending on model
Ground pressure: 0.53kg/cm² (7.55psi)
History: introduced into Czech service in 1964, the OT-62 is an improved version of the Soviet BTR 50 PK. It features a more powerful engine that gives superior performance despite the thicker armour and consequent weight increase. Access to the troop compartment is considerably eased by incorporating a large square hatch on both sides of the hull. Another distinctive feature is the incorporation of a second cupola. The OT-62(A) is normally unarmed; the OT-62(B) has a small turret on the right-hand cupola which is armed with a 7.62mm (0.31in) machine gun and an externally mounted T-21 82mm (3.23in) recoilless gun

The OT-62/TOPAS Model C is an

upengined variant of the Model B

General Motors Canada Light Armoured Vehicle - 25

Country of origin: Canada
Type: armoured personnel carrier (wheeled)
Crew: three + six
Combat weight: 12,882kg (28,400lb)
Dimensions: length of hull 6.393m (20.97ft); width 2.499m (8.03ft); height overall 2.692m (8.83ft)
Armament system: one 25mm (1in) McDonnell Douglas Helicopters M242 Bushmaster cannon; one 7.62mm (0.31in) M240 coaxial machine gun; one 7.62mm (0.31in) M60 AA machine gun or 12.7mm (0.5in) Browning M2HB AA heavy machine gun, and four smoke dischargers on each side of the turret
Armour: welded steel varying between 8-10mm (0.315-0.39in) in thickness
Powerplant: 205kW (275hp) Detroit Diesel 6V-53T diesel engine driving an 8 × 8 layout
Performance: road speed 99.8km/h (62mph), 10.5km/h (6.5mph) over water, driven by two propellers; road range 668km (415 miles)
History: the LAV-25 entered service with the USA Marine Corps in 1983 and is a derivative of the Armoured Vehicle General Purpose series, fitted with a two-man Delco turret.

The LAV-25 is available in a range of options including logistics vehicle, mortar carrier, maintenance/recovery vehicle, anti-tank and
command and control vehicles

GIAT AMX-10P

Country of origin: France
Type: armoured personnel carrier
Production: entered service in 1973
Crew: one + nine
Combat weight: 14.2 tonnes (31,240lb)
Dimensions: length 5.778m (18ft 11in); width 2.78m (9ft 1in); height 2.57 (8ft 5in)
Armament system: one 20mm (0.8in) automatic gun and one 7.62mm (0.31in) CA
Armour: welded aluminium
Powerplant: Hispano-Suiza HS 115-2 V-8 water-cooled diesel engine developing 280hp at 3,800rpm
Performance: road speed 65km/h (40.37mph), 40km/h (24.84mph) off-road, 8km/h (4.97mph) over water
History: the AMX-10P armoured personnel carrier is an amphibious, air-portable vehicle capable of good cross-country mobility. It is armed with a 20mm (0.8in) automatic gun, plus a 7.62mm (0.31in) machine gun, housed in a two-man turret located immediately to the rear of the driver's position, and above and forward of the troop compartment. Fitted with passive night-driving aids and good targeting optics, and an efficient NBC system, the AMX-10P carries a nine-man infantry section.

A useful mechanised infantry combat vehicle, which has won many export orders

Creusot-Loire AMX VCI

Country of origin: France
Type: armoured personnel carrier
Production: entered service in 1957
Crew: three + 10
Combat weight: 15,000kg (33,000lb) loaded; 12,500kg (27,500lb) empty
Dimensions: length 5.7m (18ft 8in); width 2.51m (8ft 2in); height 2.41m (7ft 10in) with turret, 2.1m (6ft 10in) to hull top
Armament system: one 7.5mm (0.3in) or 7.62mm (0.31in) or 12.7mm (0.5in) machine gun
Armour: 10-30mm (0.4-1.19in) welded steel
Powerplant: SO FAM 8 Gbx 8-cylinder petrol engine developing 250hp at 3,200rpm
Performance: road speed 65km/h (40.37mph); range 350-400km (217-248 miles); fuel 410 litres (90.3 Imp gal)
Ground pressure: 0.7kg/cm² (10.01psi)
History: a development of the highly successful AMX-13 light-tank design, the VCI has for many years been the major French armoured personnel carrier. Exported to many countries, in many versions including command post, ambulance, engineer, and mortar carrier, and an ammunition re-supply vehicle for self-propelled artillery batteries.

Developed in the early 1950s, as the basis of the AMX-13 light tank

Renault VAB VTT

Country of origin: France
Type: armoured personnel carrier
Crew: two + 10
Combat weight: 13,000kg (28,600lb) loaded; 11,000kg (24,200lb) empty
Dimensions: length 5.98m (19ft 7in); width 2.49mm (8ft 2in); height 2.06m (6ft 9in) without armament
Armament system: Creusot-Loire TLi 52A turret with a 7.62mm (0.31in) machine gun
Armour: welded steel
Powerplant: MAN D 2356 HM 72 6-cylinder inline water-cooled diesel engine developing 235hp at 2,200rpm
Performance: road speed 92km/h (57.14mph), 7km/h (4.35mph) over water; range 1,000km (621.12 miles); fuel 300 litres (66.08 lmp gal)
History: this is the French Army's standard wheeled armoured personnel carrier, which exists in both 4 × 4 and 6 × 6 layout. Fully amphibious, the VAB can carry differing armament fits depending on its role, the most common variant being the standard APC which carries a machine-gun turret.

The French Army's standard armoured personnel carrier

Berliet VXB-170

Country of origin: France
Type: multi-role vehicle
Production: entered service in 1972
Crew: one + 11
Combat weight: 12,700kg (27,940lb) loaded; 9,800kg (21,560lb) empty
Dimensions: length 5.99m (19ft 7in); width 2.5m (8ft 2in); height 2.05m (6ft 8in) without turret
Armament system: one 90mm (3.54in) gun or two 20mm (0.8in) cannon; one 12.7mm (0.5in) machine gun or two 7.62mm (0.31in) machine guns, or 81mm (3.2in) mortar, and various anti-tank missile systems and anti-aircraft missile systems
Armour: maximum 7mm (0.28in)
Powerplant: Berliet V8 diesel engine developing 170hp at 3,000rpm
Performance: road speed 85km/h (52.8mph), 4km/h (2.48mph) over water; range 750km (465.84 miles); fuel 220 litres (48.46 Imp gal)
History: the VXB is based on commercial components and intended for paramilitary rather than first-line military deployment. The all-welded construction is fully amphibious. Its crew can enter and leave the vehicle by way of side, rear and roof hatches.

The VXB 170 is based on commercial components and intended for paramilitary deployment

Panhard VCR (4 × 4)

Country of origin: France
Type: armoured personnel carrier
Production: entered production in 1978
Crew: three + nine
Combat weight: 7,000kg (15,400lb)
Dimensions: length 4.565m (14ft 11in); width 2.49m (8ft 2in); height 2.53m (8ft 3in) including armament
Armament system: one 7.62mm (0.31in), one 12.7mm (0.5in) machine gun or one 20mm (0.8in) cannon; or one 60mm (2.38in) breech-loaded mortar discharger on both sides of the hull (optional) at front and one 7.62mm (0.31in) machine gun at rear
Armour: welded steel varying in thickness between 8-12mm (0.32-0.48in)
Powerplant: Peugeot V-6 petrol engine developing 140hp at 5,250rpm
Performance: road speed 110km/h (68.32mph), 4.5km/h (2.8mph) over water; range 950km (590.06 miles); internal fuel capacity 242 litres (53 Imp gal)
History: the VCR (véhicule de combat à roues/wheeled combat vehicle) range can be used in a diversity of roles with modified armament fits and interior configurations. The basic APC carries 10 infantrymen seated on benches, five along each side of the hull, facing each other.

Panhard M3

Country of origin: France
Type: armoured personnel carrier
Production: entered production in 1971
Crew: two + 10
Combat weight: 6,100kg (13,420lb) loaded;
5,300kg (11,660lb) empty
Dimensions: length 4.45m (14ft 7in); width
2.4m (7ft 10in); height with turret 2.48m (8ft
1in), 2m (6ft 6in) without
Armament system: Creusot-Loire STB rotary
support shield with 7.62mm (0.31in) machine
gun
Armour: 8-12mm (0.32-0.48in)
Powerplant: Panhard Model 4 HD 4-cylinder
air-cooled petrol engine developing 90hp at
4,700rpm
Performance: road speed 100km/h
(62.12mph), 4km/h (2.48mph) over water;
range 600km (372.67 miles); fuel 165 litres
(36.34 Imp gal)
History: the automotive components are
almost identical to those of the AML armoured
car series. Variants include the M3/VAT repair
vehicle, M3/VDA air-defence vehicle with a
turret mounting two cannon and M3/VLA with
front-mounted dozer blades.

142 *The M3 has twin rear doors and two
more doors in the hull sides*

Thyssen Henschel/Krupp MaK Schützenpanzer Neu M-1966 Marder

Country of origin: West Germany
Type: mechanised infantry combat vehicle
Production: entered service in 1969
Crew: four + six
Combat weight: 28,200kg (62,040lb) loaded
Dimensions: length 6.79m (22ft 3in); width 3.24m (10ft 7in); height 2.95m (9ft 8in) including searchlight, 2.86m (9ft 4in) to turret top
Armament system: one 20mm (0.8in) Rh 202 cannon, elevation +65°, depression −17°, 1,250 rounds carried; two 7.62mm (0.31in) MG3 machine guns, coaxial and at rear, 5,000 rounds; six smoke dischargers on the turret
Armour: welded steel
Powerplant: MTU MB 833 Ea-500 6-cylinder diesel engine developing 600hp at 2,200rpm
Performance: road speed 75km/h (46.58mph); range 520km (322.98 miles); fuel 652 litres (143.61 Imp gal)
Ground pressure: 0.8kg/cm² (11.44psi)
History: a very important vehicle to the West German Army. It is powerful, having its own anti-armour capability with its turret-mounted MILAN ATGW missile system. The Marder A1 version was a retrofit appearing in 1981 and the A1A an upgraded version.

The Marder is the German Army's standard mechanised infantry combat vehicle

Thyssen Henschel
Transportpanzer 1 Fuchs

Country of origin: West Germany
Type: armoured personnel carrier (wheeled)
Production: entered service in 1979
Crew: two + 10
Combat weight: 17 tonnes (37,400lb) loaded; 14 tonnes (30,800lb) unloaded
Dimensions: length 6.76m (22ft 2in); width 2.98m (9ft 9in); height 2.3m (7ft 6in)
Armament system: one 20mm (0.8in) or one 7.62mm (0.31in) and six smaller dischargers
Armour: welded steel
Powerplant: 240kW (320hp) Mercedes-Benz OM 402A 8-cylinder water-cooled turbocharged diesel
Performance: speed 105km/h (65.22mph); range 800km (497 miles); fuel 430 litres (95 Imp gal)
History: the TPz 1 Eloka is an electronic warfare version fitted with EK 33 jamming equipment; the TPz1 FuFu is the command and communications version; there is a reconnaissance version, the ABC Erkundsgruppe, and there is also a battlefield surveillance version.

German standard wheeled armoured personnel carrier designed for maximum flexibility

Thyssen Henschel Condor

Country of origin: West Germany
Type: armoured personnel carrier
Production: the prototype appeared in 1978
Crew: three + nine
Combat weight: 9,800kg (21,560lb) loaded; 7,340kg (16,148lb) empty
Dimensions: length 6.06m (19ft 10in); width 2.47m (8ft 1in); height 2.79m (9ft 1in) to turret top, 2.1m (6ft 10in) to hull top
Armament system: one 20mm (0.8in) cannon, elevation +60°, depression −6°; one 7.62mm (0.31in) coaxial machine gun (optional) and two quadruple smoke dischargers, also optional
Armour: welded steel
Powerplant: Daimler-Benz OM 352A 6-cylinder water-cooled diesel engine developing 168hp
Performance: speed 105km/h (65.22mph); road range 500km (310.56 miles); fuel 280 litres (62 Imp gal)
History: the highly versatile Condor was designed to replace the UR-416. The basic vehicle can carry nine infantrymen in its APC role, or can be converted into a specialist reconnaissance vehicle with a 20mm (0.8in) cannon, or a specialist tank destroyer version with MILAN or HOT ATGWS.

This versatile type was designed to replace the widely-used UR-416

Mitsubishi Type SU60

Country of origin: Japan
Type: armoured personnel carrier
Production: entered service in 1960
Crew: four + six
Combat weight: 11,800kg (25,960lb) loaded; 10,600kg (23,320lb) empty
Dimensions: length 4.85m (15ft 10in); width 2.4m (7ft 10in); height 2.31 (7ft 6in) with machine gun, 1.7m (5ft 6in) without
Armament system: one 12.7mm (0.5in) M2 machine gun on roof, one 7.62mm (0.31in) M1919A4 bow machine gun
Armour: welded steel
Powerplant: Mitsubishi 8 HA-21 WT V-8 air-cooled turbocharged diesel engine developing 220hp at 2,400rpm
Performance: speed 45km/h (27.95mph); range 230km (142.86 miles)
Ground pressure: 0.57kg/cm² (8.15psi)
History: the SU60 has no amphibious capability or sophisticated night-vision aids. Once standard equipment in Japanese mechanised battalions, the SU60 had little tactical value and is now obsolete. There were two mortar-carrier versions developed, the SV60 and the SX60.

An obsolete APC with mortar carrier variants, the SV60 and SX60

DAF YP-408

Country of origin: Netherlands
Type: armoured personnel carrier (wheeled)
Production: entered service in 1964
Crew: two + 10
Combat weight: 12 tonnes (26,400lb)
Dimensions: length 6.32m (20ft 5in); width 2.4m (7ft 10in); height 1.18m (3ft 10in) to hull top
Armament system: one 12.7 (0.5in) machine gun; two triple barrelled smoke dischargers
Armour: maximum 15mm (0.6in)
Powerplant: DAF D5575 6-cylinder inline water-cooled turbocharged diesel engine developing 165hp at 2,400rpm
Performance: speed 80km/h (49.69mph); range 500km (310.56 miles)
History: the YP-408 lacks amphibious capability and an NBC protection system; night vision devices can be fitted, however. The PWI-S (PC) and PWCO are command vehicle variants. The PW-GWT is an ambulance vehicle, the PW-V a cargo model with a 1,500kg (3,309lb) payload, and other variants also exist.

The type lacks amphibious capabilities and an NBC protection system

BRAVIA Chaimite V-200

Country of origin: Portugal
Type: armoured personnel carrier
Crew: 11
Combat weight: 7,300kg (16,060lb) loaded
Dimensions: length 5.606m (18ft 4in); width 2.26m (7ft 4in); height 2.26m (7ft 4in) to turret top, 1.84m (6ft) to hull top
Armament system: fitted with BRAVIA turret; twin 7.62mm (0.31in), twin 5.56mm (0.22in) or one 7.62mm (0.31in) and one 12.7mm (0.5in) machine gun
Armour: 6.35-9.35mm (0.25-0.37in)
Powerplant: V-8 petrol engine developing 210hp at 4,000rpm or V6 diesel
Performance: road speed 99km/h (61.49mph), 7km/h (4.35mph) over water; road range for petrol-engined model 804-965km (500-600 miles) or for diesel-engined model 1,367-1,529km (854-955 miles); fuel 300 litres (66 Imp gal)
History: this vehicle is a licenced variant of the USA-designed Commando armoured car and APC. The Chaimite is the first armoured vehicle to be manufactured in Portugal. Optional equipment includes a number of armament additions, and night vision devices. Anti-tank, mortar-carrying and upgunned models also exist.

The Chaimite V-200 wheeled APC can be fitted with a variety of BRAVIA weapon installations

Sandock-Austral Ratel 20

Country of origin: South Africa
Type: infantry fighting vehicle
Crew: four + seven
Combat weight: 18,500kg (40,785lb)
Dimensions: length, hull 7.212m (23.66ft); width 2.516m (8.25ft); height overall 2.915m (9.56ft); ground clearance 0.34m (13.4in)
Armament system: one 20mm (0.8in) GIAT M693 (F2) cannon with 1,200 rounds; two 7.62mm (0.31in) machine guns, one coaxial and one AA, with 6,000 rounds; two smoke-dischargers on each side of the turret, and a 7.62mm (0.31in) machine gun at the hull rear
Armour: welded steel varying in thickness between 6-20mm (0.24-0.79in)
Powerplant: one 210kW (282hp) D 3256 BTXF diesel engine driving a 6 × 6 layout
Performance: road speed 105km (65.2mph); road range 1,000km (621.12 miles); fording 1.2m (3.9ft); gradient 60%; side-slope 30%; vertical obstacle 0.35m (13.8in); trench 1.15m (3.8ft); fuel 430 litres (94.5 Imp gal)
History: an extremely useful infantry fighting vehicle, with excellent range, fire power and cross-country mobility. The Ratel 60 variant is armed with a 60mm (2.36in) breech-loading mortar.

The Ratel 20 offers good range with
156 *good fire power*

Autocamiones BMR-600

Country of origin: Spain
Type: infantry fighting vehicle
Production: entered service in 1979
Crew: two + 16
Combat weight: 13,000kg (28,600lb) loaded
Dimensions: length 6.15m (20ft 2in); width 2.49m (8ft 2in); height including armament 2.36m (7ft 8in), 2m (6ft 6in) to hull top
Armament system: one 7.62mm (0.31in) machine gun, 2,500 rounds carried
Armour: welded aluminium
Powerplant: Pegaso 9157/8 diesel developing 306hp at 2,600rpm
Performance: road speed 100km/h (62.12mph), 10km/h (6.21mph) over water; range 900km (559 miles); fuel 320 litres (70.48 Imp gal)
History: the Blindado Medio de Ruedas 600 was developed to meet the requirements of the Spanish Army, which until this time had relied upon obsolescent USA equipment. The vehicle is fully amphibious, being propelled in the water by two DOWTY water jets mounted on the rear of the engine deck. An unusual feature of the BMR-600 is its hydropneumatic suspension, which allows the driver to adjust the vehicle's ground clearance to suit the ground conditions.

This wheeled infantry fighting vehicle has a remotely-controlled 12.7m (0.5in) machine gun

Hagglund & Soner
Pansarbandvagn 302

Country of origin: Sweden
Type: infantry fighting vehicle
Production: entered service in 1966
Crew: 2 + 10
Combat weight: 13,500kg (29,700lb) loaded
Dimensions: length 5.35m (17ft 6in); width 2.86m (9ft 4in); height 2.5m (8ft 2in) including turret, 2.06m (6ft 9in) to hull top
Armament system: one 20mm (0.8in) cannon, elevation +50°, depression −10°, 505 rounds carried; two quadruple smoke grenade launchers
Armour: welded steel
Powerplant: Volvo THD 100B 6-cylinder inline turbocharged diesel engine developing 280 hp at 2,200rpm
Performance: road speed 66km/h (40.99mph), 8km/h (4.97mph) over water; road range 300km (186.34 miles); fuel 285 litres (62.78 Imp gal)
Ground pressure: 0.6kg/cm² (8.58psi)
History: the Pansarbandvagn 302 is the standard armoured personnel carrier of the Swedish Army. Fully amphibious, the vehicle is equipped with a powerful Hispano Suiza cannon for use against both ground and airborne targets. Many variants of the basic vehicle exist, including a command post model, designated Stripbv 3021.

The PVB-302 has no facility for personal weapons to be fired

BMP-1

Country of origin: USSR
Type: mechanised infantry combat vehicle
Crew: three + eight
Combat weight: 13,500kg (29,700lb) loaded; 12,500kg (27,000lb) empty
Dimensions: length 6.74m (22ft 1in); width 2.94in (9ft 7in); height 2.15m (7ft)
Armament system: one 73mm (2.89in); one 7.62mm (0.31in) coaxial; one SAGGER ATGW launcher
Armour: welded steel varying in thickness between 6-33mm (0.24-1.3in)
Powerplant: 300bhp D 6-cylinder water cooled
Performance: road speed 80km/h (49.69mph), 8km/h (4.97mph) over water; range 500km (310.56 miles); fuel 460 litres (101 Imp gal)
Ground pressure: 0.57kg/cm² (8.12psi)
History: armed with the low-powered 73mm (2.89in) 2A28 smooth-bore gun housed in the same one-man turret as used on the BMD, this amphibious vehicle has many sophisticated assets not normally found on Soviet vehicles, but requires better fire power. The crew has good visibility and improved targeting aids.

The primary armoured personnel carrier for the infantry units within Soviet tank divisions

BMP-2

Country of origin: USSR
Type: tracked mechanised infantry combat vehicle
Crew: three + seven
Combat weight: 14,600kg (32,187lb)
Dimensions: length overall 6.858m (22.5ft); width 3.089m (10.135ft); height 2.077mm (6.81ft)
Armament system: one 30mm (1.2in) 2A42 cannon; one 7.62mm (0.31in) PKT coaxial machine gun; one launcher for AT-5 'Spandrel' anti-tank missiles and three smoke dischargers on each side of the turret; the turret is electrically powered; the main gun lacks stabilisation but an optical fire-control system is fitted; the type can also generate smoke by injecting fuel into the exhaust system
Armour: welded steel with appliqué steel on the turret sides
Powerplant: 300kW (402hp) Model 5D20 diesel engine
Performance: road speed 80km/h (49.7mph); 7km/h (4.3mph) over water driven by its tracks; road range 500km (311 miles); fording amphibious; gradient 60%; vertical obstacle 0.7m (2.3ft); trench 2.5m (8.2ft); fuel 460 litres (101 Imp gal)

Developed from the baseline BMP-1, the BMP-2 entered service in the late 1970s

BMD-1

Country of origin: USSR
Type: airborne combat vehicle
Crew: seven
Combat weight: 8,000kg (17,600lb) loaded
Dimensions: length 5.41m (17ft 8in); width 2.55m (8ft 4in); height 1.77m (5ft 9in)
Armament system: one 73mm (2.89in) gun, elevation +33°, depression −4°, 40 rounds carried; three 7.62mm (0.31in) PKT machine guns, coaxial and two bow; one SAGGER ATGW launcher with three missiles
Armour: 6-25mm (0.24-0.99in)
Powerplant: V-6 liquid-cooled diesel engine developing 290hp
Performance: road speed 80km/h (49.69mph), 10km/h (6.21mph) over water; range 320km (198.76 miles) fuel 300 litres (66.08 Imp gal)
Ground pressure: 0.6kg/cm² (8.72psi)
History: a highly innovative vehicle, the airportable BMD armoured support vehicle offers protection from small-arms fire to its crew and passengers. Equipped with the low pressure 73mm (2.89in) gun and the SAGGER anti-tank missile, the vehicle offers airborne troops a valuable fire-support facility.

The BMD-1 is only lightly protected, to ensure a high measure of air portability

BTR-50 P

Country of origin: USSR
Type: armoured personnel carrier (tracked)
Crew: two + 20
Combat weight: 14,200kg (31,240lb)
Dimensions: length 7.08m (23ft 2in); width 3.14m (10ft 3in); height 1.97m (6ft 5in)
Armament system: one 7.62mm (0.31in) machine gun
Armour: 10-14mm (0.4-0.55in)
Powerplant: Model V-6 6-cylinder inline water-cooled diesel engine developing 240hp at 1,800rpm
Performance: road speed 44km/h (27.33mph), 11km/h (6.83mph) over water; range 400km (248.45 miles); fuel 400 litres (88 Imp gal)
Ground pressure: 0.51kg/cm² (7.27psi)
History: developed in the middle of the 1950s from the PT-76 amphibious light tank chassis, the BTR-50 P was the Soviet Army's standard tracked armoured personnel carrier, until replaced by the BMP-1. Standard equipment includes some night-vision equipment, and for a D-44 field gun to be loaded. This is not available to the BTR-50 PA. The BTR-50 PK is an improved version affording cover to the troops; many other variants exist.

The BTR-50P was the Soviet Army's standard tracked APC, being
replaced by the BMP-1

GKN Defence MCV-80 Warrior

Country of origin: UK
Type: mechanical infantry combat vehicle
Production: entered service in 1986
Crew: three + seven
Combat weight: 20,000kg (44,000lb)
Dimensions: length 5.42m (17ft 8in); width 2.8m (9ft 2in); height 2.82m (9ft 3in) including turret; ground clearance 0.5m (1ft 7in)
Armament system: one 30mm (1.2in) Rarden cannon, one 7.62mm (0.31in) coaxial machine gun; two quadruple smoke dischargers
Powerplant: Rolls-Royce CV8 TCE-8 diesel engine developing 800bhp at 2,300rpm
Performance: maximum speed 75km/h (46.6mph); range 500km (310 miles)
History: the driver is seated front left, with the engine compartment to the right. The two-man turret is central, with the troop compartment at the rear. The infantry are unable to use their small arms from within. The MCV-80 carries a full range of passive night-vision equipment. Variants include a platoon command vehicle, mortar carrier, artillery command post, all with GPMG turrets, and an engineer combat repair vehicle.

The Warrior is the UK's first true mechanised infantry combat vehicle

GKN Defence FV 432

Country of origin: UK
Type: tracked armoured personnel carrier
Crew: two + 10
Combat weight: 15,280kg (33,685lb)
Dimensions: length overall 5.25m (17.23ft); width 2.80m (9.19ft); height including machine gun 2.29m (7.5ft); ground clearance 0.41m (1.33ft)
Armament system: one 7.62mm (0.31in) L7A2 cupola-mounted machine gun and three smoke dischargers on each side of the hull front; an alternative fit is one 7.62mm (0.31in) L7A2 machine gun and four smoke dischargers on each side of an electrically-powered lightweight turret
Armour: welded steel varying in thickness between 6-12mm (0.24-0.47in)
Powerplant: 179kW (240hp) Rolls-Royce K60 Mo.4 Mk 4F multi-fuel engine
Performance: road speed 52.3km/h (32.5mph), 6.6km/h (4.1mph) over water driven by its tracks and supported by a flotation screen; fording 1.07m (3.5ft) gradient 60%; vertical obstacle 0.61m (2ft); trench 2.06m (6.75ft); fuel 454 litres (100 Imp gal)

Evolved from the FV 420 series of armoured vehicles which failed to enter production in the 1950s, the FV 432 armoured personnel carrier appeared in the early 1960s

Alvis Stormer

Country of origin: UK
Type: armoured personnel carrier
Crew: three + eight
Combat weight: 10,689kg (23,516lb) loaded
Dimensions: length 5.3m (17ft 4in); width 2.654m (8ft 7in) with appliqué armour, 2.374m (7ft 8in) without; height 2.374m (7ft 8in); ground clearance 0.362m (1ft 2in)
Armament system: one 20mm (0.8in) or 30mm (1.2in) cannon; one 76mm (3in) or 90mm (3.56in) gun and twin 20mm (0.8in) AA
Armour: welded aluminium
Powerplant: Perkins T6/3544 6-cylinder turbocharged diesel engine developing 200bhp at 2,600rpm
Performance: road speed 72km/h (44.72mph), 6.5km/h (4.04mph) over water; road range 800km (497 miles); fuel 405 litres (89.2 Imp gal)
Ground pressure: 0.37kg/cm² (5.29psi)
History: the Stormer was developed from the Spartan APC and incorporates a longer hull which is also very slightly wider. Alvis purchased the manufacturing rights in 1980 and named the vehicle Stormer in 1981. It is fully amphibious, and is fitted with a full range of night-vision equipment.

Developed from the FV 4333, the Stormer is available in a very wide range of options

Alvis FV 603 Saracen

Country of origin: UK
Type: armoured personnel carrier
Production: began 1952; ended 1972
Crew: two + 10
Combat weight: 10,170kg (22,374lb) loaded
Dimensions: length 5.233m (17ft 2in) overall; width 2.539m (8ft 4in); height 2.463m (8ft 1in); ground clearance 0.432m (1ft 5in)
Armament system: two 7.62mm (0.31in) machine guns, one in turret, elevation +45°, depression −15°, one on ring mount at rear, 3,000 rounds carried; two smoke dischargers
Armour: welded steel varying in thickness between 8-16mm (0.32-0.64in)
Powerplant: Rolls-Royce B80 Mk 6A 8-cylinder petrol engine developing 160hp at 3,750rpm
Performance: road speed 72km/h (44.7mph); range 400km (248.5 miles); fuel 200 litres (44 Imp gal)
Ground pressure: 0.98kg/cm² (14psi)
History: the FV 603 takes full advantage of shared components in common with the Saladin armoured car and FV 622 Stalwart high-mobility load carrier. Variants include the FV 603 (C) Saracen Mk 3 with reverse-flow cooling for operation in hot climates; the FV 604 Command Post without turret and the FV 611 ambulance.

The first post-war generation of
light armoured fighting vehicles

Cadillac Gage Commando V-300

Country of origin: USA
Type: multi-role armoured vehicle
Production: entered service in 1983
Crew: three + nine
Combat weight: 12,700kg (27,940lb)
Dimensions: length 6.4m (20ft 11in); width 2.54m (8ft 3in); height 2.692m (8ft 9in) including turret; ground clearance 0.533m (1ft 8in)
Armament system: one-man turret with twin 7.62mm (0.31in) MGs, or one 7.62mm (0.31in) and one 12.7mm (0.5in) MG; or one 20mm (0.8in) cannon and coaxial 7.62mm (0.31in) MG; or two-man turret with one 76mm (3in) gun and coaxial 7.62mm (0.3in) MG; or one 90mm (3.56in) and coaxial 7.62mm (0.31in) MG
Armour: welded steel
Powerplant: V-8-555 diesel engine developing 250bhp at 3,000rpm
Performance: speed 88.51km/h (55mph), 4.8km/h (3mph) over water; range 644km (400 miles); fuel 284 litres (62.56 Imp gal)
History: developed from the Commando V-150 series, the 6 × 6 Commando V-300 offers superior cross-country capabilities. Options include an NBC protection system, night vision and air-conditioning, and a very wide range of armament. Variants under development include an anti-tank version with TOW missiles.

A development of the 4 × 4
178 *Commando V-150 series*

Cadillac Gage Commando V-150

Country of origin: USA
Type: multi-role armoured vehicle
Production: entered service in 1964
Crew: three + nine
Combat weight: 9,888kg (21,754lb)
Dimensions: length 5.689m (18ft 7in); width 2.26m (7ft 4in); height 1.981m (6ft 5in) over hull; ground clearance 0.381m (1ft 2in)
Armament system: pintle-mounted 7.62mm (0.31in) machine gun
Powerplant: 151kW (202hp) Cummins diesel engine
Performance: road speed 88km/h (54.66mph), 4.8km/h (2.98mph) over water; range 643km (399 miles); fuel 303 litres (67 Imp gal)
History: numerous variants are available in addition to the APC detailed above, which replaced both the much lighter, 7,371kg (16,250lb) original V-100 and the stretched V-200. Main variations centred on turret type.

Variants include a one-man unit with a 20mm (0.8in) cannon

FMC M2 Bradley

Country of origin: USA
Type: tracked infantry fighting vehicle
Crew: three + seven
Combat weight: 22,590kg (49,800lb)
Dimensions: length overall 6.453m (21.17ft); width 3.2m (10.5ft); height 2.565m (8.42ft) to turret roof; ground clearance 0.43m (1.6ft)
Armament system: one 25mm (1in) McDonnell Douglas Helicopters M242 Bushmaster cannon; one 7.62mm (0.31in) M240C coaxial machine gun; one retractable two-tube launcher with seven TOW missiles, and two smoke dischargers on each side of the turret
Armour: welded aluminium, aluminium appliqué and laminate
Powerplant: 373kW (500hp) Cummins VTA-903 diesel engine
Performance: road speed 66km/h (41mph), 7.2km/h (4.5mph) over water driven by its tracks; road range 483km (300 miles); vertical obstacle 0.91m (3ft); trench 2.54m (8.33ft)

Designed as a mechanised infantry combat vehicle for the USA Army from the early 1960s, this series originated with the XM701 experimental vehicle of 1965 and the Armored Infantry Fighting Vehicle of 1967 onwards

Autocar/Diamond T/ International Harvester/White M3A1

Country of origin: USA
Type: armoured half-track vehicle
Crew: 13
Combat weight: 9,298kg (20,456lb) loaded; 6,940kg (15,268lb) empty
Dimensions: length 6.337m (20ft 9in); width 2.22m (7ft 3in); height 2.692m (8ft 9in); ground clearance 0.28m (11ft)
Armament system: one 12.7mm (0.5in) M2HB machine gun, one 7.62mm (0.31in) machine gun
Armour: welded steel varying in thickness between 7-13mm (0.28-0.51in)
Powerplant: White Motor Company engine, developing 147bhp at 3,000rpm
Performance: road speed 73km/h (45mph); range 321km (199 miles); fuel 227 litres (50 gal)
History: manufactured in great numbers during World War II. Still widely used in South America, the Middle East and Japan, the many variants included the M2 half-track car produced in the late 1950s, M4A1 81mm (3.19in) mortar carrier and many rebuilds for Israel using the 128kW (172hp) Detroit Diesel 6V-53 diesel engine.

The M3 has enhanced anti-tank capabilities

MC M113A1

Country of origin: USA
Type: tracked armoured personnel carrier
Crew: two + 11
Combat weight: 11,156kg (24,595lb)
Dimensions: length overall 4.863m (15.95ft); width 2.69m (8.81ft); height 2.5m (8.2ft)
Armament system: one 12.7mm (0.5in) Browning M2HB cupola-mounted heavy machine gun; the cupola is manually powered, the gun lacks stabilisation in either elevation and simple optical sights are fitted
Armour: welded aluminium varying in thickness between 12.7-38.1mm (0.5-1.5in)
Powerplant: 157kW (210hp) Detroit Diesel 6V-53N diesel engine
Performance: road speed 67.6km/h (42mph), 5.8km/h (3.6mph) over water driven by its tracks; road range 483km (300 miles); fording amphibious; gradient 60%; vertical obstacle 0.61m (2ft); trench 1.68m (5.5ft); ground clearance 0.41m (1.33ft); fuel 360 litres (95 USA gal/79 Imp gal)
History: development started in 1956, since when 14,815 of the baseline M113 and 16,160 vehicles of the standard M113A1 have been produced, in addition to the numerous other variants

FMC LVTP7

Country of origin: USA
Type: armoured amphibious assault vehicle
Production: began 1971; ended 1974
Crew: three + 25
Combat weight: 22,838kg (50,244lb) loaded, 17,441kg (38,370lb) empty
Dimensions: length 7.94m (26ft); width 3.27m (10ft 8in); height 3.26m (10ft 8in) overall; ground clearance 0.406m (1ft 3in)
Armament system: one 12.7mm (0.5in) M85 machine gun, elevation +60°, depression −10°, 1,000 rounds carried
Armour: 10-45mm (0.4in-1.78in)
Powerplant: Detroit Diesel Model 8V53T 8-cylinder engine developing 400hp at 2,800rpm
Performance: road speed 64.31km/h (40mph) 13.5km/h (8.39mph) over water; road range 482km (300 miles); fuel 681 litres (150 Imp gal)
Ground pressure: 0.57kg/cm² (8.15psi)
History: variants include the upgraded LVTP7 with a Cummins VT904/400 engine, passive night-vision equipment, smoke-generating capability and an automatic fire detection and suppression system, designated LVTP7A1, and the LVTC7 tracked landing vehicle designated the Command Model 7, which has shelter-erecting capabilities and a crew of 13.

Improved variants include the
LVTP7A1, with a new diesel engine

and infrared equipment. Russian tanks all have an ability that their NATO counterparts do not have – that of snorkelling or wading a river totally submerged. This is because the Russians believe that in war, tanks would have to cross a great number of rivers, often without bridges.

A further Russian tank development is the T-64/72, which has a 125mm (4.9in) gun firing APFSDS, HEAT-FS and HE-FRAG FS from a smooth-bore gun, with an automatic loader, which enables the crew to be reduced to three men. From the T-64/T-72 has come a development which is the equal of the modern NATO-produced tanks: the T-80, based on the T-64. With additional ceramic armour added to its turret, it incorporates a 125mm (4.9in) smooth-bore gun, an HVAPFSDS, with further research into a Depleted Uranium (DU) round. In common with NATO tanks, the T-80 has been equipped with passive night-vision equipment, a laser rangefinder and a full-solution ballistic computer, as well as having full stabilisation on the main armament.

At the same time as main battle tanks were being introduced, the need for a lighter vehicle for reconnaissance purposes was recognised, one that would not be heard or seen but with enough offensive weaponry to protect itself. Britain and France led the way, producing respectively the Saladin and the AMX-13 tank.

A line of Scorpions, typical of today's
fighting vehicles

(4.7in) gun, intended to have a fire-control system equal to that envisaged by the USA's partners in NATO and to have the same protective armour as the British Challenger.

One major problem faced by crews is that of space – storage of ammunition, equipment and tools – and ensuring that equipment does not jam the turret traverse area; also, to ensure that they have enough food and water to survive if necessary in a nuclear environment, enclosed in their tanks. Fatigue is another problem; especially tiring are the night operations, where a man's effective observation limit is one hour, using modern sights. Comfort is also important, as a crew moving rapidly across an uneven terrain can emerge shaken and bruised, often with serious injury resulting from rapid cross-country movement.

During the period when NATO was developing its new generation of tanks, the USSR was carrying out a similar programme. After the heavy and powerful JSIII and T-10 came the considerably lighter T-54/55, at 36 tonnes. Later came the T-62, a development of the T-54/55 series. Probably over 40,000 T-62s were produced either in the USSR or in factories in its territories. The T-62 weighed 40 tonnes and was armed with a 115mm (4.5in) gun. The early T-62 was relatively unsophisticated; however, later developments included laser rangefinders

The Brazilian ENGESA EE-T1 Osorio
6 *MBT, first seen in prototype in 1984*

Index

Introduction

The world's major nations have a strong force of main battle tanks supplemented by light tanks which are used for reconnaissance purposes. A main battle tank is a heavily armoured mobile gun platform capable of engaging other tanks and vehicles at ranges of up to 10km (6.2 miles). Since the conclusion of World War II, tank development has reached technological levels then undreamt of. The British Centurion which was designed in 1944, and introduced into service in 1949, proved its value in the Korean War, where it was able to defeat the Russian T-34/85. Still in service with the Israeli Army nearly forty years after its introduction, it was probably the first modern tank.

The continual technological developments have led to more sophisticated optical devices, improved firepower, better communications and more protection for crews.

In 1952 the Americans introduced the M48 into service and it remains in service to this day. A further improved version was introduced in 1960 as the M60 and has gone through various modifications. In 1971 the USA instituted a research programme which resulted in the production of the M1 Abrams, using a 120mm

The Chinese NORINCO YW 53, seen here firing a Red Arrow-8 ATGW, is used in great numbers and several
4 *variants by the Chinese Army*

Contents

First published in England 1993 by
Wordsworth Editions Ltd
Cumberland House
Crib Street
Ware
Hertfordshire SG12 9ET

ISBN 1 85326 995 6

Photographs by courtesy of TRH Pictures and Guy
Taylor, London

Set in 8$\frac{1}{2}$/9pt Monophoto Univers
Text conversion and pagination by
August Filmsetting, St Helens

Printed in Italy by Amadeus s.p.a.

A WORDSWORTH COLOUR GUIDE

VEHICLES

Wordsworth Editions